An Introduction to Puppets and Puppet-making

An Introduction to Puppets and Puppet-making

DAVID CURRELL

MALLARD
PRESS

MALLARD PRESS

An imprint of BDD Promotional Book Company, Inc.
666 Fifth Avenue, New York, NY 10103

Mallard Press and the accompanying duck logo are
registered trademarks of the BDD Promotional Book
Company, Inc. registered in the US patent and
trademark office. Copyright © 1992.

First published in the United States of America
in 1992 by the Mallard Press

ISBN 0-7924-5724-2

This book was designed and produced by
Quintet Publishing Limited
6 Blundell Street
London N7 9BH

Project Editor: Stefanie Foster
Creative Director: Richard Dewing
Designer: Stuart Walden
Editor: Michelle Clark
Photographer: Ian Howes
Additional Photography: Martin Norris

Special thanks to Pippa Howes who modeled and
painted the puppets' heads.

Typeset in Great Britain by
Central Southern Typesetters, Eastbourne
Manufactured in Singapore by
J. Film Process Singapore
Printed in Singapore by
Star Standard Industries (P.T.E.) Ltd

To my wife, Ayla.

Contents

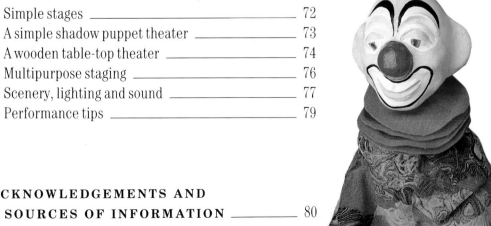

Introduction

The puppet and the puppet theater are unique. A puppet is not an actor and a puppet theater is not human theater in miniature, because while an actor *represents*, a puppet *is*. It brings to the performance the essence of the character and no more; it has no identity outside its performance, so brings no other associations to the stage. It is this quality of the puppet and the power with which it conveys character and emotion that have attracted the attention of such artists as Edward Gordon Craig, Jean-Baptiste Molière, Jean Cocteau, Paul Klee and George Bernard Shaw.

The puppet theater therefore has great scope as a liberating performance art. The puppet is free from human limitations and scale – it can even be non-human in form. The fascinating nature of the puppet and the compelling way in which it attracts and sustains attention are clearly major reasons for its popularity through 4000 years, both as a folk art and, at times, a fashionable craze or high art.

Much of the early history of puppet theater is conjecture, but its origins are thought to lie mainly in the East. Later it flourished in the early Mediterranean civilizations, toured Europe with wandering showmen in the Middle Ages and was used in churches to portray the scriptures. Since the Renaissance it has had an unbroken tradition in Europe, from where, in the nineteenth century, emigrants took their national traditions to America and established the foundations for today's great variety of styles.

Modern performance methods are now found in most countries, sometimes alongside ancient traditions where there have been mutual influences in the development of puppet theater, human theater, mime and dance. Indeed, in many respects, puppetry has more in common with mime and dance than with human theater. Television puppetry has revived popular interest in the art, but puppet theater is to be found also in the home, in live theater, and for education and therapy.

This book aims to introduce the reader to the principles of puppetry and to facilitate the making and manipulation of characters of a high standard through carefully arranged steps with easy-to-follow instructions.

ABOVE: Puppets are thought to have originated in the East, and these Javanese shadow puppets are an example of a long-standing tradition.

ABOVE: Modern puppetry has come a long way, and a huge variety of puppets and performances exist all over the world.

TYPES OF PUPPET

SHADOW PUPPETS

Shadow puppets are cut-out figures held between a source of light and a translucent screen. They can form solid silhouettes or be decorated with various amounts of cut-out details. Color can be introduced into the cut-out shapes to provide another dimension. Full-color, translucent figures enable a clear image to be presented in whatever pose the puppet is designed.

For effective characterization, shadow puppets tend to have parts in profile and parts turned toward the audience. Javanese shadow puppets are the classic example of this, where the parts of the body are arranged like ancient Egyptian illustrations. The head, legs and feet are in profile, but the body is partially turned toward the audience. The arms hang in front of and behind the puppet.

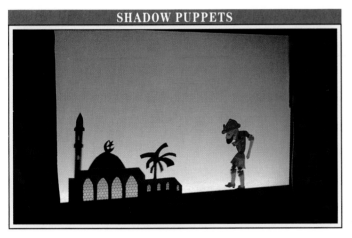

SHADOW PUPPETS

HAND PUPPETS

Glove puppets are so-called because they consist of a head with a mitten-type glove body. Such a puppet may have separate shaped hands, legs and feet, though normally the puppet will be visible only to the hips. The glove must be long enough to ensure that your arm does not show while performing so it should reach almost to your elbow; your wrist forms the puppet's waist.

A mouth puppet is a large head with moving mouth. Often it is attached to a tube-shaped body into which you insert your arm, effecting mouth movements with your fingers in the head and your thumb in the lower jaw. Your free hand becomes the puppet's hand. The lion puppet illustrated on page 38 is an example.

ROD PUPPETS

Rod puppets are constructed around a central rod secured in the head. It may be attached so that the head can nod, turn or do both. The body can range from a simple shoulder block with loose robes to a complete torso and pelvis with a full costume. Arms may vary from a piece of rope to fully joined limbs, and the hands are controlled by strong wires. Legs are not essential, but may be added if necessary.

MARIONETTES

Marionettes are fully articulated figures. The head and neck can be made in one piece, but are generally better if jointed; the torso, pelvis and limbs reflect the human figure and joints, but not to human proportions.

A marionette is manipulated by means of wooden controls, held either horizontally or vertically. They look more complicated than they really are, as most of the strings are there to support the puppet; the movements are achieved to a large degree by the overall movement of the control, and the momentum and natural movement of the puppet itself. You *do* operate individual strings, but not as much as you would think.

HAND PUPPETS

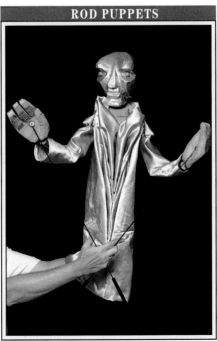

ROD PUPPETS

MARIONETTES

MATERIALS AND TECHNIQUES

USING PUPPET-MAKING MATERIALS

Foam rubber, styrofoam, paste and paper, plastic filler and cheesecloth, and plastic wood may be used for heads, hands and feet for hand puppets, rod puppets and marionettes. Bold, clear features are best, as they have the maximum impact and are visible to your audience. Used in an appropriate thickness, the materials are strong *and* lightweight. Explore each of the materials as shown later in the chapter and persevere if they do not behave exactly as you expect at first, as they can take a while to master.

Sculpting foam rubber or styrofoam involves starting with a block and deciding what to cut away in order to achieve the character. If you happen to change your mind, it is possible to glue pieces back on, so try it and see rather than being too tentative.

Modeling using the other malleable materials mentioned above allows you to get the structure right in a basic form and then to add to it and shape it as desired.

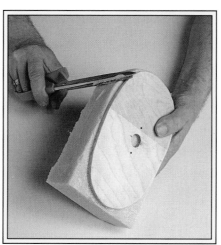

NOTE

Each project in the following chapters specifies particular materials as examples, but these techniques and materials are frequently interchangeable, so do explore the possibilities of each. Do also read through the projects carefully before embarking on any of them, as most of them need specific tools and equipment. These include such workshop tools as a vice, jigsaw or coping saw, chisels, rasps, drills, etc. Make sure you have everything you need before you begin making a puppet, or you may be caught out!

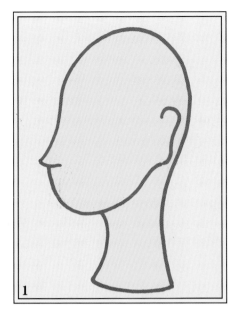

1 Make glove puppet heads with slightly bell-shaped necks or with a small ridge around the edge to enable you to secure the glove body to it without it slipping off. Make the hole inside the neck oval big enough for two fingers.

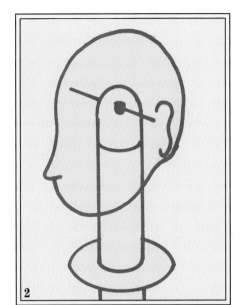

2 You can make a basic rod puppet head with a neck, but if it is to nod, build the neck onto the body with a joint inside the head.

3 Marionette heads can be made with or without a neck, but they move most effectively when the neck is separate from both head and body and jointed inside each.

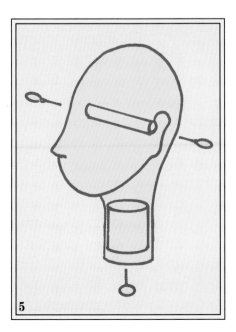

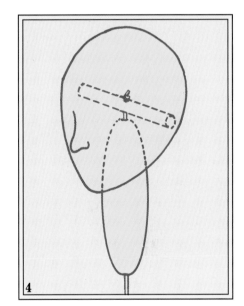

4 Also, the ears should be strong enough to attach the head strings to. If they are not, you will need to secure a dowel rod (⅜in./9mm in diameter) through the head to which you can fix screw-eyes. If the head and neck are separate, you will need to drill a hole through the center point of the dowel so that you can secure a cord to the neck.

5 If the head and neck are in one piece, secure a short length of 1-in. (25-mm) diameter dowel in the neck so you can attach a screw-eye in order to join the head to the body.

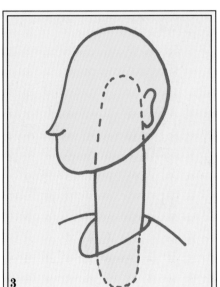

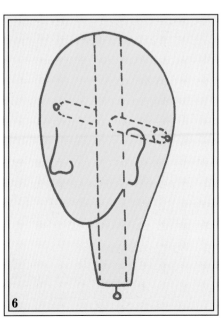

6 If, however, the head and neck are sculpted from foam rubber or styrofoam, use two lengths of dowel made into a cross by drilling a hole through a long vertical dowel to accommodate a smaller horizontal dowel. Glue and insert the larger dowel into the neck; then do the same for the smaller rod, through the head.

SIZE

Before setting about making a puppet (or a whole cast of puppets), first decide on your performance and the most appropriate *type* of puppet. Now you can determine how many puppets you need, how they must look and what they must be able to do, so that you can build these elements into your designs. The puppets and stage need to be large enough to be seen clearly, but not so big that they will not fit into the available performance space and, where appropriate, transportation. If they are too light, they will not operate well; on the other hand, if they are too heavy, manipulating and transporting them will be difficult.

Because of these factors, rod puppets and marionettes tend to be between 18 and 30in. (45 and 75cm). The size of glove puppets is determined by the fact that they must fit your hand. Shadow puppets may be any size, but bear in mind that they must fit the shadow screen *and* have plenty of room to move.

PROPORTION

With some exceptions, puppets modeled on human proportions look odd; a common problem is to make them too tall and thin. You need to exaggerate the head, hands and feet. Making the puppet's head about one fifth of its height often looks best, but choose the size that suits the purpose.

Typically, the size of the hand will be the distance from the chin to the middle of the forehead so that it can cover most of the face. This is also the length of the forearm. A foot will be a little longer than this.

Elbows are usually level with the waist, wrists with the crotch, and fingertips halfway down the thigh. The body is normally a little shorter than the legs.

Placing the eyes approximately halfway up the head, one eye's width apart, with the ears approximately level with the eyes and the end of the nose is in keeping with human scale.

Experiment with proportions, too – variation is important.

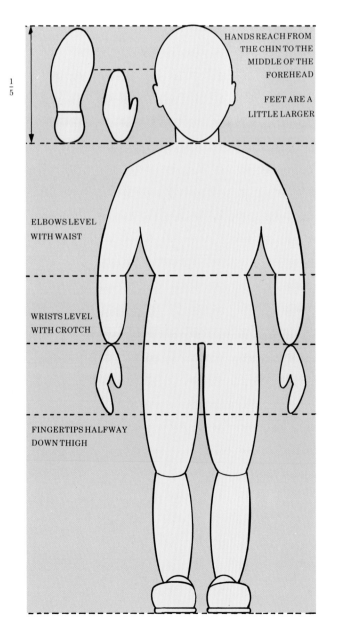

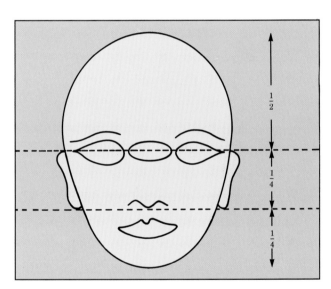

When designing your puppets, consider the head. Experiment. See what happens when you take an egg shape and make it spherical, then lengthen it, flatten it, make it into a pear shape, invert it.

Add a nose and ears, change the position of the nose on the face (moving the ears so that they align with the nose), and change the size of the nose.

Enlarge the chin, reduce the chin, enlarge the forehead, make the face more angular, and change the angle of the chin.

Set the eyes more deeply, enlarge the eyes, vary the distance between the eyes, and change the shape and size of the mouth. Consider, too, the areas of light and shade that are created by deep modeling and by the angles of the face.

Above all, keep it simple, both for the sake of strong characterization and because fine detail will not be visible to an audience even a short distance away.

The shapes of the hands and feet are also important in creating character. Detailed modeling is unnecessary for the same reasons as before, but the hands should be held in an expressive manner so that they do not appear flat and lifeless. Look at people's hands; you will see that the fingers are not all held in the same plane, and the thumb is set in a different plane from the fingers. Though this is so, simple shaping or stylized design is effective. It is not uncommon, for example, for puppets to have only three fingers and a thumb. Also, the style of painting can give life to comparatively simple hands, as can be seen from some examples in this book.

Remember that it is not only the head, hands and feet that matter but also the overall body shape, as this contributes significantly to character. Also think about the angle of the head in relation to the body. How does changing the angles of the head or the body shape alter character?

SCULPTING HEADS

FOAM RUBBER

Foam rubber is easy to sculpt into any body part if you have suitable tools. Try a bread knife (preferably an electric one), a hacksaw blade, a craft knife or sharp scissors with large plastic handles. Some foams can be finished very effectively with a small rasp. Use good-quality foam, or it will crumble with the passage of time; make sure, too, that it is flame retardant. Use a suitable adhesive for the foam you are using; otherwise, it will melt the foam. Glue guns are ideal, but take care because the emerging glue is very hot. Ozone-friendly spray glues are now available for foam, too. The lion puppet is made of foam rubber – refer to page 38 for this technique.

MAIN STAGES IN SCULPTING A HUMAN HEAD

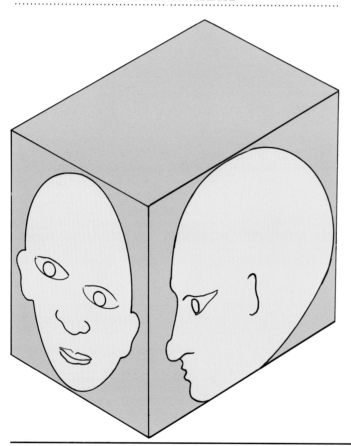

If dowel rods are to be inserted (for rod puppets or marionettes), make deep holes with a long, thin, coarse, round file; then glue the rods in place in the foam rubber. Eyes may be sculpted, but, for the best results, carve out eye sockets, then paint and varnish wooden balls of the appropriate size and glue these into the sockets. When painting foam, use spray paints for an even finish over large areas, but for small areas, mix reasonably thick paint and apply it to the foam with your fingertips – a brush makes the foam too wet.

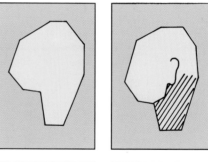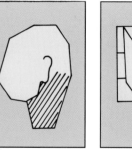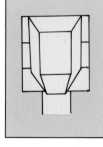

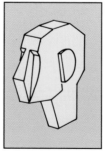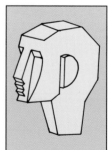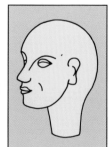

STYROFOAM

Styrofoam (polystyrene) is suitable for making heads and padding out the body. This material can be shaped easily by melting or cutting it with a saw or breadknife, but be sure that the room in which you work is well ventilated if you apply heat because toxic fumes are released when you do this. In the picture (right), you can see a rasp is being used to shape the head, and this is an ideal way of sculpting styrofoam.

Heads need to be covered with layers of paper and glue to make them strong, so make sure that your sculpting is bold and sufficiently deep, or the detail will be lost when the covering is applied. The rod puppet on page 42 uses styrofoam.

MODELING HEADS

PASTE AND PAPER

Using paste and paper is a cheap and easy method for modeling a head and you can achieve fine detail. You need to cover the clay model with damp tissue to act as a separator. Use white glue or cellular wallpaper paste, but with the latter you must allow each layer to dry before applying the next. When dry, the head is cut open and the clay is removed; the head is then rejoined with glue and other layers of paper and white glue. For this method in action see page 34.

PLASTIC WOOD

Plastic wood is suitable for making heads, hands and feet. It can be worked rather like clay, but it sets hard and can be cut, drilled and sanded like wood. If it is moistened with acetone (nail varnish remover), it is easier to model and the finish is smoother when it dries. Use acetone in a well-ventilated room and keep it away from sources of heat. Clear contact glues can be used to fix pieces together and to attach hair or whatever. The puppet's head on page 53 is made using this technique.

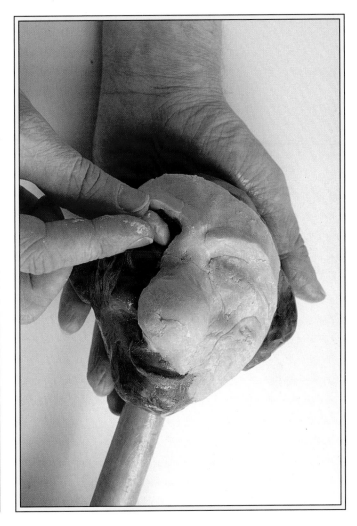

PLASTER FILLER AND CHEESECLOTH

Plaster filler is best bought in powder form and mixed with water to form a paste (always add the powder to the water). Cheesecloth (mull) impregnated with plaster filler is stronger than paste and paper for heads, and it stretches well over modeled details. An alternative is to use pieces of the plaster-impregnated bandage used by hospitals for setting broken limbs. This needs only to be dipped in water and applied to the puppet. Again, the head is modeled over a clay base on a modeling stand, and split and rejoined in the same way as for the head using the paste and paper technique. See the puppet on page 30 for this technique.

HANDS AND FEET

Before making the hands and feet, you must plan the whole
puppet and be clear about what joints you are going to use so
that you can build the appropriate ones into them.

WOOD

A simple wooden hand may be shaped from a small block of
wood. Sketch the outline shape on the block. Hold the block
firmly in a vice and use a rasp to remove the excess wood
around the hand shape. Reposition the wood to allow you to
shape the back and palm of the hand and give shape to the
fingers. Details may be added by using smaller files and chisels.

Wooden feet are made in the same way.

PLASTIC WOOD

Plastic wood hands are excellent. Once you have established
the basic shape, you can carve, file or sand it or build it up with
more plastic wood.

Intertwine pipe cleaners and establish the basic positions of
the fingers and thumb. For strong wrist joints, *either* glue a
short length of dowel into the palm of each hand *or* build a loop
of wire into the hand. Cover the pipe cleaners and dowel or wire
with clear contact glue and then add plastic wood in fairly large
pieces. Do not try to attach it to individual fingers, but make a
larger pad and then snip between the fingers with scissors.
Model the shape of the fingers, smoothing them with acetone as
you do so. When the plastic wood has dried, build up or cut
away the plastic wood as necessary and finish.

Plastic wood feet are modeled on balsa wood.

Using a rasp and/or craft knife, establish the basic shape of
the foot in balsa wood. Cover the balsa wood with clear contact
glue; then cover it with plastic wood, modeling it until you have
the right shape. When the plastic wood has dried, build up or
cut away the plastic wood if necessary and finish.

FOAM RUBBER

First establish the basic shape with large, sharp scissors. Then
create more detailed shaping with smaller scissors. Always
make small snips or the scissors will hurt your fingers after a
short while.

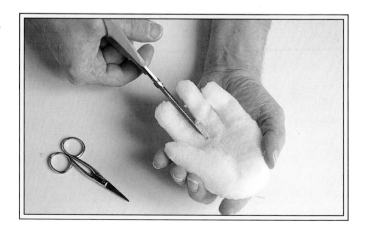

BODY STRUCTURE

There are many ways of assembling puppets' bodies, and some
examples of the methods used in this book are shown below.
These puppets display different techniques, but remember
that you can vary them, and use your own ideas, too.

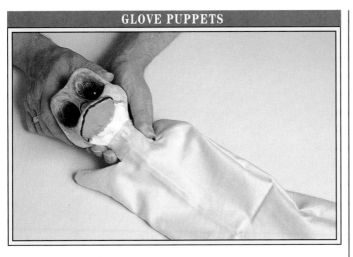

The body of a glove puppet is the glove itself.

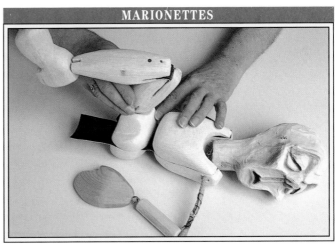

This marionette is composed of several shaped parts, and the
arms use a combination of techniques.

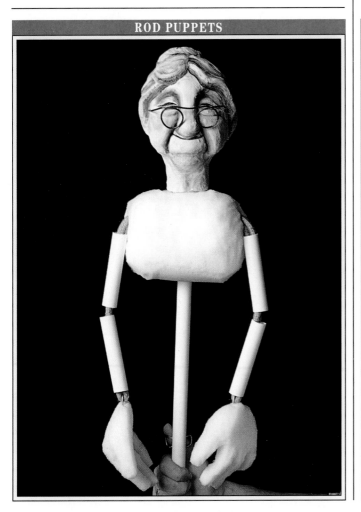

This rod puppet's body uses a central control inserted through a
block of foam, and the arms have been jointed using rope
inserted through two separate hollow tubes.

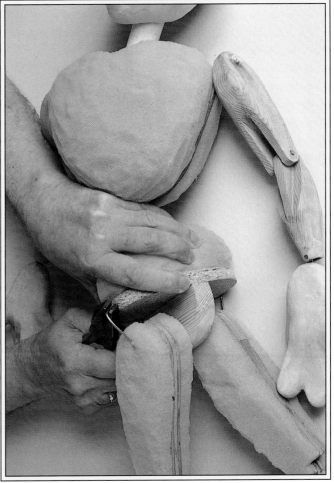

The arms of this puppet are made of jointed, carved sections,
while the upper body and legs use foam-covered flat wooden
sections to emphasize their shape.

PAINTING AND DRESSING THE PUPPET

PAINTING

It is a good idea to paint the head, hands and feet at the same time and after all the necessary joints have been constructed. Try to avoid giving the pieces a glossy finish as this is distracting and unnatural, especially under lighting, as it reflects the light.

There is a wide variety of paints available, so explore the possibilities, but acrylic paints will suit most needs. When mixed with acrylic medium, they have a slightly shiny finish; but if you mix them with water, they have an appropriate matt appearance. When mixing larger quantities that require a lot of white, latex paint is an economical substitute.

Use acrylic varnish to give shine to those parts that need it, such as eyeballs and, perhaps, the lips. When the varnish is wet, it looks milky, but do not be alarmed, it dries *clear*.

Sometimes, rather than using a paintbrush, it is better to apply the paint directly with your fingers.

Spray paints are useful for large puppets and are particularly useful for painting on foam rubber.

When it comes to what and how to paint, everything depends on what you are trying to achieve and the style of the performance you are planning; but, as a general rule, you should consider delineating the face in the style of stage make-up. Look at the head under, and allow for, any lighting that you intend to use. Remember that if you paint protruding parts too dark a color or recessed areas in colors that are too light, you will neutralize the effect of your modeling and detract from the characterization.

There are no fixed rules for face colors – anything is possible – but if you need normal flesh colors as a base, mix white, yellow, red and brown in varying amounts to achieve the desired shade. Premixed flesh colors are seldom satisfactory, but can be a useful base.

Pure white eyeballs can be very stark, so a slightly creamy color will often be preferable. However, it is sometimes very effective to paint the whole eyeball in a deep color such as purple, blue, green or black, or to insert into the eye socket a varnished colored wooden ball or bead.

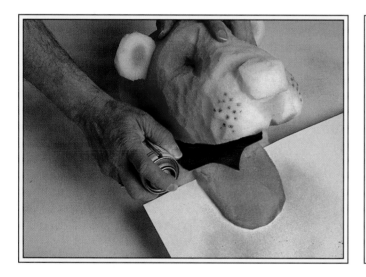

HAIR

Hair may be modeled and painted, but it usually looks very much better if suitable materials are either glued directly to the head, or a wig is made and then glued on. Good materials to use are rope or string (dyed if necessary), knitting or rug yarn, fur fabric, curled cardboard and even wood shavings.

Artificial hair pieces (for example, pony tails) and so on, can be used, but the less realistic materials are easier to use and more in keeping with the nature of the puppets. Eyebrows may be painted on or made from the same material as the hair.

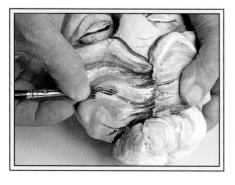

The puppet's costume contributes significantly to its character, so design it carefully; the costume on the glove puppet duck transforms the appearance of the basic glove. Remember that, like other aspects of puppet theatre, it is often the clean, simple lines that are the most effective. When period costumes are needed, research them thoroughly and try to identify the essential characteristics of the period.

There is a further important dimension to a puppet's costume: you will find that the movement of the costume can enhance the movement of the puppet itself. This is a major consideration in the choice of fabrics, as different fabrics create very different effects. If you make sure that your fabric is full enough, it will have some movement or "life" of its own. Jersey fabric, cut on the bias, is excellent for full, flowing robes.

It is of paramount importance, however, that the fabrics be soft and reasonably lightweight, so that they do not impede the movements of the puppet. But remember that if they are too thin, light will show through.

Consider not only the combination of colors but also the combination of textures: puppets all dressed in the same type of fabric will look very boring. Avoid large prints as these are inappropriate for small puppets. You might need to dye fabric to achieve the color needed in a particular material, and you can paint or stencil patterns onto plain fabric with textile paints or very thin acrylic paint.

If you intend to use colored lighting, remember that the lights will have an effect on how different-colored fabrics appear, so it is a good idea to test swatches of material under the lighting before proceeding.

It is a mistake to conceive puppet costume as if you were dressing a doll. In particular, the inside edges of seams on close-fitting garments can be very restricting. You might find it helpful, therefore, not to make the costume as a suit of clothes, but to create it directly on the puppet.

If you are sewing the costume, trim the seams carefully. A quick and easy alternative to sewing is to glue the costume together; you will need to add the occasional stitch to any points subject to strain, as shown here for the glove puppet's pants legs. A clear contact glue is suitable for most materials.

You can construct the costume in similar shapes to human clothes, but remember that simple draped fabrics can be much more interesting and appropriate for some puppets. See the puppet on page 67 for guidance with more detailed costume. Do also keep a collection of trimmings for the costumes: braids, fringes, ribbons, lace, buttons and beads, costume jewelry, etc. But avoid anything that will catch or snag, especially when making costumes for marionettes.

ABOVE: Quite a lot of rich fabric is sewn directly onto the puppet.

RIGHT: A very light, flowing fabric, which will not impede movement, has been used for the clown.

LEFT: More detailed costume has been sewn and glued onto this marionette, and the buttons pick up on the facial coloring and that of the clothes.

BELOW: Stark colors have been used for the duck's costume, which is sewn and glued together.

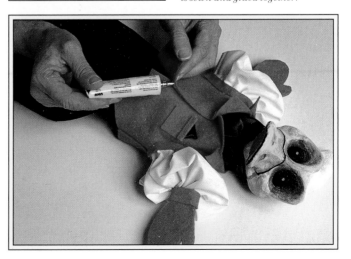

METHODS OF MANIPULATION

Illustrated below are the various ways of manipulating the
puppets that are described in this book.

*W*ire controls or dowel rods are used to control shadow
puppets.

*F*or hand puppets, the hand provides direct control inside the
head or glove.

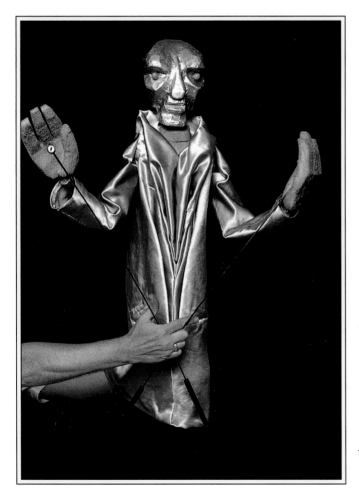

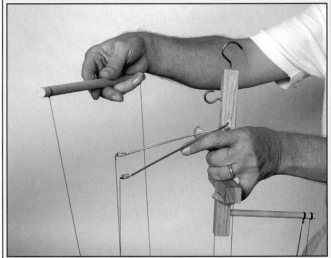

*A*irplane and upright controls are used to manipulate the
strings on marionettes. The control illustrated is an upright
one.

*R*od puppets require the use of both hands: one for an inside
mechanism to control the nodding and turning of the head
and the movement of the body, while the other hand is used to
manipulate control wires attached to the hands.

1

Shadow Puppets

—

A Simple Shadow Puppet

MATERIALS

Shadow puppets are normally flat, cutout figures held by a rod or wire and illuminated against a translucent screen, hence their name. Traditionally made of parchment or hide, now they are usually made from cardboard.

For a simple silhouette, black is ideal but not essential. Any fairly strong cardboard, such as that from a cereal box, will make a good puppet. Think about the size of your puppets in relation to the size of the screen, leaving space for all actions.

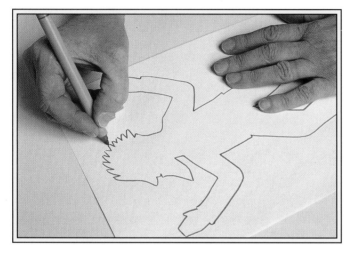

1 Transfer the design on paper onto cardboard. I make the puppets up to 12in (30cm) high for a screen that is 27½in (70cm) high.

2 Cut out the shape with sharp scissors for a clean outline. You can stiffen the cardboard by coating it with white glue.

3 Hold the puppet gently between your thumb and index finger, adjusting the position to find the point of balance. Attach the control rod slightly above this point, so that there is a little more weight below the control rod than above it to make sure that the puppet remains naturally upright, rather than tending to somersault as you operate it.

4 For the control rod, you need a 12-in (30-cm) length of ⅜-in (9-mm) diameter softwood dowel. Secure the rod to the puppet with a thumbtack, just above the point of balance. You will need to tap the thumbtack in securely to make sure the puppet turns with the rod and does not swing uncontrolled. With this type of control rod, the puppet cannot turn around, but it is very easy to make a duplicate facing in the opposite direction.

TIPS FOR STRENGTHENING A PUPPET

If part of a puppet needs strengthening, glue a piece of clear acetate over the weak part. Then cut the acetate to follow the outline of the part.
Alternatively, it may be possible to put the puppet parts through a laminating machine.

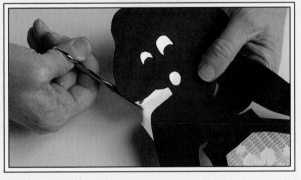

DECORATION

You can add to the design of your shadow puppets by cutting out decorative or key shapes within the outline using a sharp craft knife or small, pointed scissors or by punching holes. You will find it helpful to study Javanese *wayang kulit* shadow puppets and Chinese figures, as they use cutout decoration to superb effect. Remember that these figures are made of leather that can hold its shape even when much of it has been removed, but do not cut away too much of your cardboard figures or they will be too weak to withstand a performance!

As an alternative to cutting out intricate decorations, you can cut away larger areas and cover the exposed sections with suitably textured materials that allow light to show through the design – for example, nets, lace or paper doilies.

ABOVE: *Here lace has been used to add detail to the skirt.*

ABOVE: *Colored translucent acetate adds to the effect of this puppet.*

A Jointed Shadow Puppet

Jointed shadow puppets are very effective, but do keep them simple. By all means joint parts that can achieve their effect by swinging freely or where you can effect some degree of influence over their movement through the operation of the main control rod. However, it is a mistake to make a jointed puppet that needs lots of control wires.

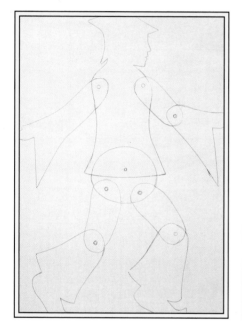

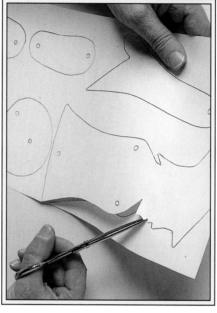

1 Draw the silhouette figure on paper. Draw clearly the overlapping parts where you want to make a joint.

2 Copy the design on another sheet of paper with all the parts drawn in full without overlapping so that you can cut out a pattern for each part.

3 Draw around your templates onto a sheet of stiffish, smooth cardboard. Cut out the separate parts.

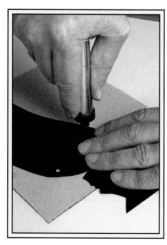

4 Use a paper punch to make clean holes at the center point of the overlapping parts. A simple stationery punch is suitable for use near the edge of the cardboard, but further in you might need a single hole punch, as illustrated.

5 Lay the overlapping parts on top of each other. Do not join them in a fashion that will permit them to catch in position. For the joint use either knotted thread or brad-type paper fasteners. If the puppet is normally to be used facing in one direction, make the joints with the head of the fastener on the screen-side of the puppet. Press the ends as flat as possible against the cardboard without restricting movement.

6 *If the fasteners have long, split ends, bend the points back in toward the center as shown in order to reduce the possibility of snagging.*

7 *Secure a dowel control rod with a thumbtack (see page 20). Attach it to the body if there is no neck joint, or to the head if the neck is jointed.*

KNOTTED THREAD JOINT

Dacron braided nylon fishing line makes an excellent alternative to paper fasteners. Pull it over beeswax before use to prevent it from fraying.

Using a large-eyed needle, push the thread through the center point of the overlapping parts and knot it on each side of the joint; make sure that the knots are close enough to the surface for the joint to be reasonably tight, but not too tight – it should move freely and smoothly.

Seal the knots with clear contact glue.

Instead of using a dowel control on shadow puppets, you can use a control wire, which gives good control and can be raised or lowered as necessary to permit operation from behind or below, making rear projection lighting techniques possible.

For this method use a piece of galvanized wire (coathanger wire) and a length of dowel for a handle. The control rod is usually attached to the body, but if the puppet has a neck joint, the control must be attached to the head; generally having head *and* body controls makes the puppet too difficult to handle.

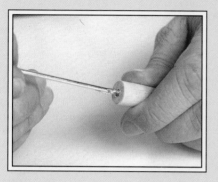 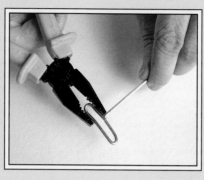 

1 *Drill a small hole into a piece of dowel approximately 3in (7.5cm) long. Glue one end of the wire securely into the hole.*

2 *Bend the other end of the wire into an elongated loop.*

3 *Secure the loop to the puppet with a piece of cardboard, stepped as shown, gluing it to the puppet.*

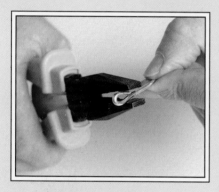  

4 *If additional controls are needed, for example for a hand, use a piece of galvanized wire, make a small loop in the end and seal the closure with glue.*

5 *Knot one end of a piece of thread, use a needle to take the other end through the cardboard, from the side facing the screen, and attach this end to the loop of wire.*

6 *With large puppets you can use the traditional technique of actually picking up the hand and holding it against the screen.*

TIP

If you need to restrict movement of the joints – for example, to prevent double-jointed movement – link the moving parts with thread which limits the degree of movement possible.

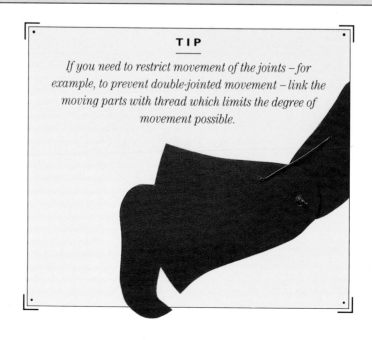

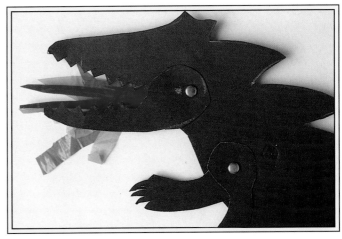

Color can be introduced to the shadow puppets and scenery by covering cutout designs with pieces of colored acetate, cellophane paper (such as candy wrappers) or tissue paper. Simply glue them to the surrounding area of the back of the puppet. This can produce wonderful results in enhancing the appearance of clothing.

Particularly effective is a combination of translucent color and textured fabric, such as lace or gauze.

SCENERY

Keep scenery simple: unless it is translucent, every piece of scenery cuts down on the acting area for the puppets. Make black scenery with shapes cut from stiff cardboard.

Moving scenery such as doors may be secured with a hinge of fabric glued in place. Tape a piece of wire to the moving part for easy operation. If the puppet needs to walk on the scenery, glue small strips of wood onto the back of the scenery for the puppet to walk on.

A Full-Color Translucent Puppet

It is possible to use modern materials in ways akin to the traditional oriental methods applied to leather, treating it to make it translucent and coloring it with dyes. For some time puppeteers have imitated the traditional puppets using lampshade parchment tinted with inks to very good effect, but more recently another technique has become very popular for producing full-color translucent puppets. Plain white cardboard is colored, then treated with oil to make it translucent.

To achieve this effect yourself, use good-quality cardboard – Ivory Board is recommended and the best weight is 335g/m². If your board is too thin, the puppet will be too floppy; if it is too thick, it will not be sufficiently translucent.

1 *First, draw the design on paper, then draw it lightly on the white cardboard (remember that, if it is to be articulated, you must draw all the parts separately, allowing for the overlaps). Do not cut out the parts at this stage.*

2 *Color the puppet with felt pens or radiant concentrated watercolors as described opposite.*

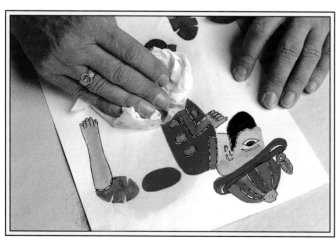

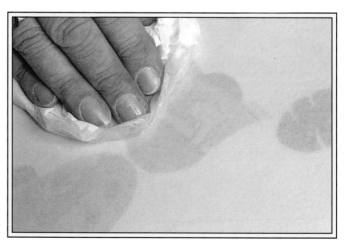

3 *Make sure your work surface has protective covering if needed. To make the cardboard translucent, rub it with paper towel soaked in either cooking oil or preferably, because it is cleaner, clear liquid paraffin (available from druggists). First, treat the colored side, rubbing the oil right* in. *The cardboard will tend to curl upward very slightly at the edges on the side you oil first, which is helpful if you oil the colored side first as suggested as it means that the edges of the puppet will remain flat against the screen when held by the control rod.*

4 *Turn over the cardboard and rub oil into the other side. In a very short time the color will appear on this side, too. When all the color shows through and the cardboard is fully translucent, wipe away any excess oil using clean paper towel. It is easy to see if any parts have been missed, but,* *if you are in any doubt, hold the cardboard up to the light and you will see darker, rather grayish patches if you have missed an area.*

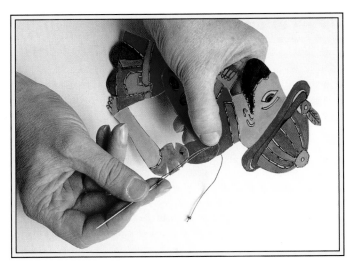

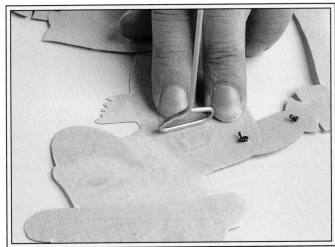

5 *Cut out the puppet and join any moving parts. This is done now rather than earlier to avoid* *causing any damage while you are oiling the puppet.*

6 *Add the control rod and any additional controls if they are needed. It has to be accepted that normally the attachment of the controls will show – you can even build this in to your design. If, however, you wish to make them* *less visible, you can attach a main control wire either with thread, or with a piece of clear acetate. Use clear contact glue (you may have to experiment to find a suitable glue as not all glues will adhere to the oiled surface).*

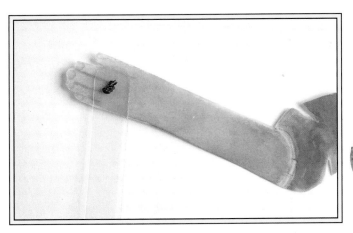

7 *A strip of clear acetate, attached by means of a knotted thread joint, may be* *used in place of additional control wires.*

USING FELT PENS

Use either water- or spirit-based pens. Spirit-based colors tend to merge where the colors meet, giving at first a very subtle effect, though in time it is possible for the colors to *continue* merging and for the detail to be lost. Water-based colors, on the other hand, remain clear and crisp, but the price you pay is that the effect is more stark. Whichever type of pen you use, completely fill in blocks of color – light shading with separate lines of color is not effective.

USING RADIANT CONCENTRATED WATERCOLORS

Paint on the cardboard with radiant watercolors (or diluted transparent dyes). Dr. Martin Radiant Concentrated Water Colors or a comparable alternative are recommended. These colors do not mix to produce exactly the colors that are produced by mixing paints, and diluting them with water produces very different effects again.

CONTROL AND MANIPULATION

It is common practice to attach the main control rod to the body or to the head if it moves.

Additional control rods may be added if necessary, but you will achieve greater effect and variety if you keep the method of control simple. A main control rod and one additional wire are usually sufficient.

Too many control rods or wires will be impossible to operate, and the effect will be destroyed, not enhanced. Shadow puppets are particularly good at inviting the audience to imagine dimensions or actions not possible with two-dimensional puppets. All you have to do is suggest and let the rest of the playing happen in their imaginations.

The illustrations exemplify just how much control can be exercised over a puppet's entire body movements from the manipulation of one control rod. Make use also of the screen itself. As you operate the puppet, slight pressure against the screen can help you to maintain a puppet's pose and you can use the frame as a ledge on which to walk the puppet.

If you need the puppet to do something very specific, but infrequently, it is best to make a duplicate just for that effect. Similarly, if you need a particular gesture, such as a pointing hand, simply cut out a duplicate lower arm, fix it on a wire and hold it in position while the arm attached to the puppet hangs out of sight.

Unless you are using projection methods for your lighting or you wish to achieve a ghosting effect, keep the puppets close against the screen at all times to achieve a very sharp, clear image. Horizontal control rods make it easier to do this, but the puppet cannot turn around. You can, however, make a duplicate facing in the opposite direction. You cannot use horizontal control rods if you are projecting straight at the screen as you will then be standing in the way of the light, but for any other type of lighting, horizontally controlled puppets are recommended.

Vertical control wires, by contrast, allow the puppet to turn and permit a wide range of projected effects, but it is harder to keep them close to the screen while you are manipulating them. In unskilled hands they are somewhat more limited in their variety of movement, and control from a single main rod is less easily achieved.

BELOW *Here dowel rods are being used to manipulate the shadow puppets.*

RIGHT *A few simple turns of the wrist while holding the control wire can effect a whole series of movements.*

PROJECTED SCENERY

Scenery may be projected by placing cutout shapes on an overhead projector or by making your own transparencies with acetates and felt pens or translucent, colored, self-adhesive masking film. You can also photocopy (and enlarge or reduce) photographs onto Xerox acetate sheets and project the images.

2

Hand Puppets

—

A Standard Glove Puppet

MAKING THE HEAD

Make the head using one of the techniques outlined in the
Introduction. The example illustrated here uses cheesecloth
and plaster filler.

1 *Make a modeling stand by screwing a large piece of dowel to a block of wood. Make sure that the base is wider than the puppet head so that it does not tip over during modeling.*

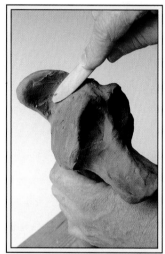

2 *Create a clay model on the stand. Remember that the neck needs to be oval to accommodate two fingers and slightly bell-bottomed.*

3 *Cover the head with dampened tissue paper, making sure the head is completely covered.*

4 *Dip small squares of cheese-cloth into the plaster filler and apply at least three layers to the head, overlapping the pieces.*

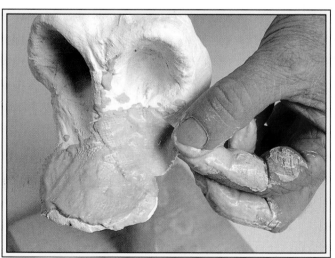

5 *Add a little colored paint to the plaster for alternate layers to ensure full coverage. Press each layer firmly into the previous one (you do not need to wait for each to dry). Detail can be added with a cotton ball saturated in plaster.*

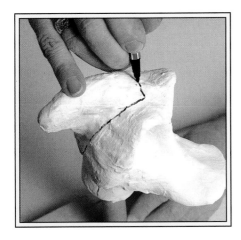 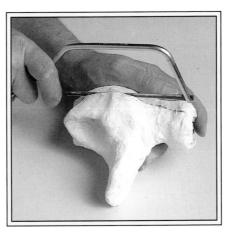 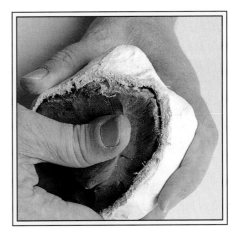

6 *When it is dry, mark a line over the head as a guide for cutting the head open with a V-shape on the top to guarantee the accurate engagement of the head when it is rejoined.*

7 *Carefully cut open the head with a junior hacksaw or a craft knife.*

8 *If necessary slice through the clay base with a piece of strong thread or wire and carefully remove the clay with an old spoon, rolling the clay away from the shell with your fingers to avoid pressure against it.*

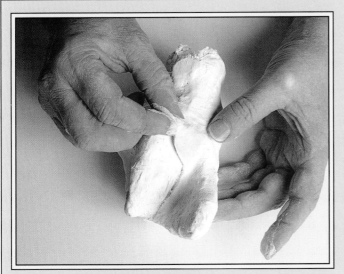 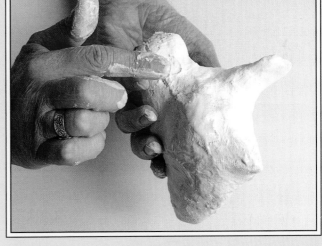

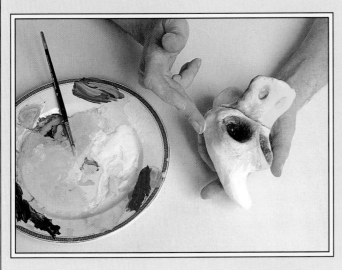 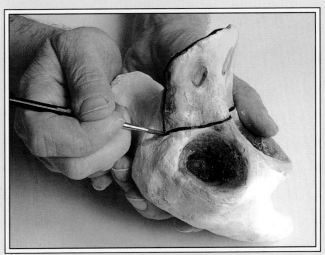

9 *Rejoin the two shells with glue and another layer of cheesecloth dipped in plaster filler. When dry, further shaping and smoothing are possible with a craft knife or fine sandpaper.*

Line the inside and edge of the neck with fabric, if necessary, to improve comfort. Finally, paint the head and add any hair.

MAKING THE BODY OF THE PUPPET

Not all costume materials are easy to fashion to the required shape and some need protection from too much wear. For this reason it is an excellent idea to make a basic glove from curtain lining, unbleached calico or a jersey material (which has a little elasticity in it) and then to glue or sew the costume itself onto this glove.

MAKING A LINING GLOVE

You will need a paper pattern, but how you make this depends on whether you will always be using the puppet on the same hand or whether you will be using it on either hand. Make sure that, when it is stitched, the neck of the glove is wide enough to fit over the puppet's neck and that the body is wide enough for your hand to slip in and out easily.

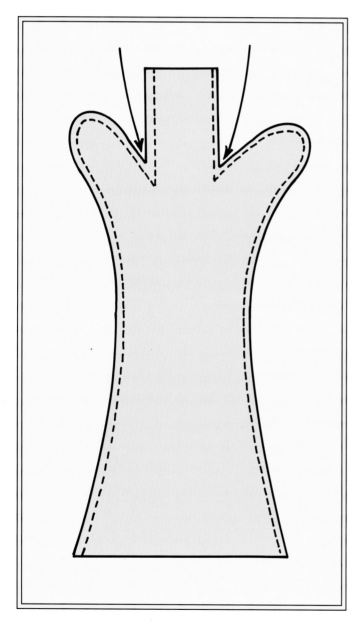

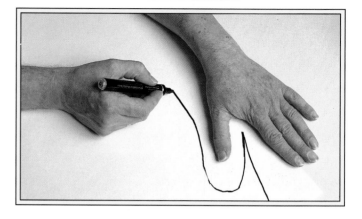

1 *For a puppet that you will use on just one hand, make the pattern for the lining glove by folding a sheet of paper in half lengthways, placing your hand on it as shown and drawing around* *your hand, allowing a margin of approximately ³⁄₄in. (2cm) around your hand and 1¹⁄₄in. (3cm) on each side of your arm. Keep this template once you are comfortable with it.*

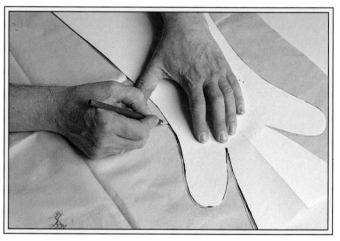

2 *Cut out the appropriate paper pattern and lay it on a double thickness of the lining material (right sides together) and draw round the pattern. If you need a* *particularly wide neck, pin a tuck in the fabric before tracing the pattern onto it. (After stitching together, remove the pins to open the tuck.)*

GLOVE FOR USE ON EITHER HAND

For a puppet that you will use on on either hand, proceed as above, but in addition, turn your hand over and draw around your hand in this position. Then make a smooth curve around both shapes, and the glove will fit a left *or* right hand.

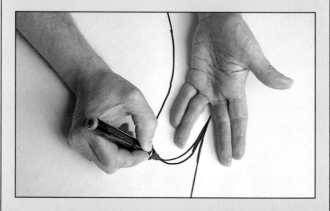

3 *By hand or machine, stitch both layers of the material together, as shown by the dotted line (do not stitch across the neck* *or the bottom of the glove). Do not cut around the shape yet.*

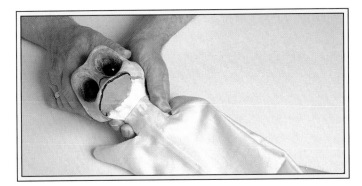

4 Try the glove for comfort on one or both hands, as appropriate. If necessary, rip out and restitch. When you have a shape that is comfortable, cut out the glove ¼in (6mm) away from the stitches. Snip into the corners between the neck and arms, right up to (but not through) the stitches so that the fabric does not pucker when the glove is reversed. Now reverse the glove so that the seams are inside. Glue it to the puppet's neck and bind it in place with a strong draw-thread.

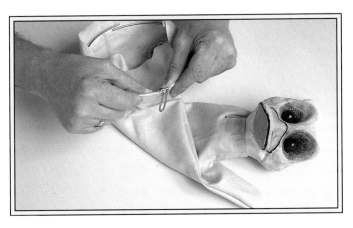

5 Take a length of 12–14 gauge galvanized wire (coathanger wire) that measures the same as the bottom edge plus enough for a loop. Bend it into a circle and a loop as shown. Stitch or glue the wire into the hem of the bottom edge of the glove. This holds the glove open so you can put the puppet on easily with one hand during a performance when you will not have both hands free. The loop enables you to hang the puppet up on a rod inside the stage so you can insert or remove your hand while performing.

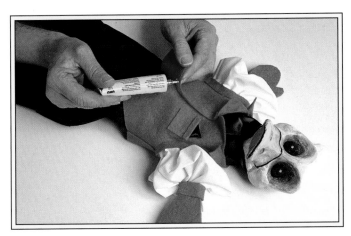

6 Finally, choose fabrics for the puppet's costume that are in keeping with its character, adding any trimmings required, and glue or stitch the costume to the lining glove. Here the basic mitten-shaped hands have been covered with pieces of hand-shaped felt.

A Glove Puppet with Hands, Legs and Feet

This puppet has larger hands than the simple mitten type that are created as part of the glove itself. With separate hands you will need to practice a little more to produce expressive gestures, and it is best to make them solid to enable you to handle props more easily. The basic glove puppet is made in the same way as the previous puppet.

MAKING THE HEAD

The head here is made using the paste and paper technique: the key stages are outlined below. Remember to splay the neck slightly at the bottom, and make sure that it is wide enough to accommodate two fingers.

1 *Model the shape in clay on a modeling stand. Keep the modeling bold, as fine detail will be lost in the following process. Remember that the neck needs to be slightly bell-bottomed.*

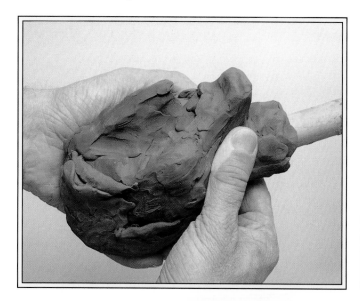

2 *Insert ear-shaped pieces of cardboard into the clay to help strengthen the ears.*

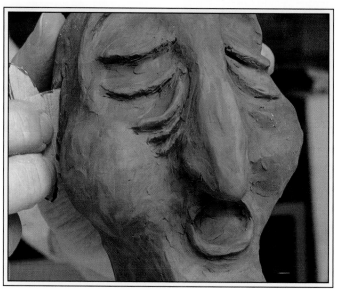

3 *Cover the clay with overlapping 1in. (25mm) squares of dampened tissue paper to prevent the head shell from sticking to the clay. Do not cover the cardboard ears.*

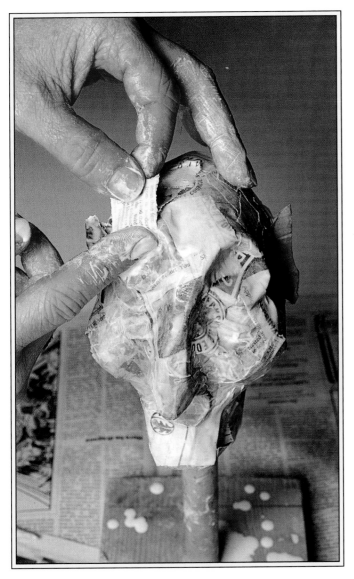

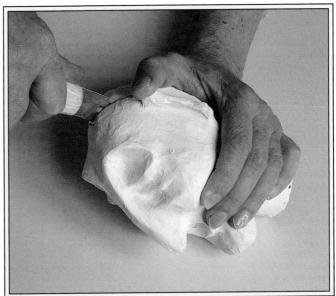

4 Apply at least four layers of newspaper, in squares, using white glue or cellular paste; alternate colors to ensure full coverage. To develop your modeling, work the detail with tissue paper rather than newspaper as it is more easily molded to shape. If you are using cellular paste, allow each layer to dry before you apply the next.

5 When it is thoroughly dry, you might apply a coat of white latex paint to add strength. Carefully cut open the head with a craft knife or junior hacksaw; cut a V-shape on top of the head so that the head parts engage accurately when rejoined.

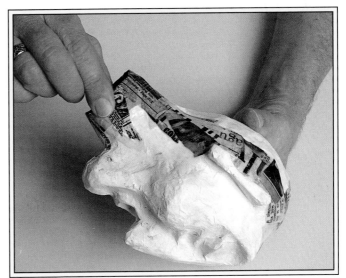

6 If necessary, slice through the clay with strong thread or wire. Carefully remove some of the clay from the center with an old spoon, then roll the clay away from the shell into the space.

7 Rejoin the hollow shells with glue and cover the head with another layer of paper and glue and a coat of latex paint. Line the inside and edge of the neck with fabric if necessary to improve comfort.

MAKING THE HANDS

The hands are made with short wrists which fit onto the puppet's arms. The wrists are hollow to accommodate your fingers or thumb. A simple wooden hand may be shaped from a small block of wood and a "cuff" added for the wrist.

1 *Sketch on the block the outline shape of the hand with a short wrist. Secure the block in a vice and remove the waste around the hand with a rasp or chisel. Add detail with a chisel, craft knife and files, then smooth with sandpaper.*

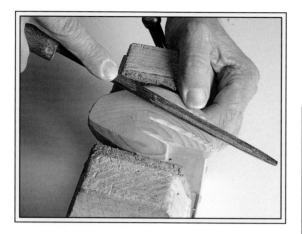

2 *Form and glue a piece of cardboard into a slightly conical tube, one end of which must fit snugly over the wooden wrist and the other end must take your first two fingers. Glue the tube to the wrist, smear it with clear contact glue and add a layer of plastic wood to give it strength. Make sure that the plastic wood is also attached to the wooden hand and plug the joint between cardboard and wrist inside the tube. When it is dry, smooth and finish the plastic wood as described in the Introduction.*

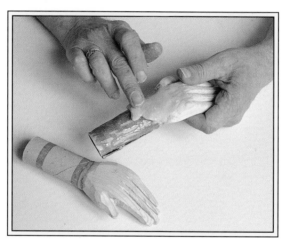

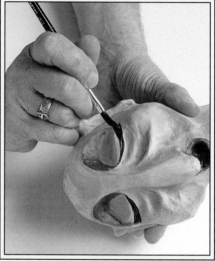

3 *Paint and finish the head and hands in keeping with the required character.*

MAKING THE BODY OF THE PUPPET

Make the glove from neutral-colored fabric so that any areas that show do not stand out too much. Curtain lining material has been used here.

1 *Make a paper pattern, ensuring that the glove reaches down to your elbow and that the neck is wide enough to secure to the head and hands. Draw around the pattern on a double layer of the glove fabric and stitch the fabric together. Do not stitch across the neck or the opening of the glove.*

2 *Cut the excess fabric away, ¼in (6mm) from the stitching and turn the glove right side out so that the seams are inside. Glue the glove to the outside of the puppet's neck, turning in the top of the material. If necessary, secure with a draw thread. Glue the puppet's cloth arm into the wooden wrist. Glue or stitch into the hem of the glove a loop of 12–14 gauge galvanized wire to allow easy insertion and removal of your hand.*

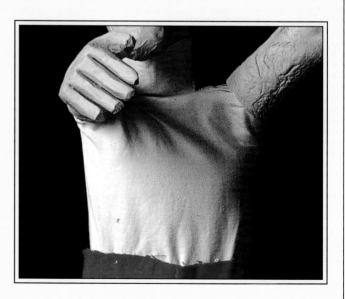

MAKING THE LEGS AND FEET

1 *Secure the pieces of wood in turn in a vice and shape two lower legs and two feet using a rasp. Create the detail using a craft knife and small files and smooth the whole shape with fine sandpaper. Glue the feet to the lower legs and further secure them by inserting a screw or nail up through the heel into the leg (drill a small guide hole first to ensure that it goes in straight). Paint the feet.*

Most glove puppets do not have legs or feet. Some characters, however, like the traditional Mr. Punch, may need legs. But, remember, you will have to hold the puppet significantly higher for the legs to show.

Make the feet from blocks of wood, the lower legs from thick dowel and the thighs from fabric.

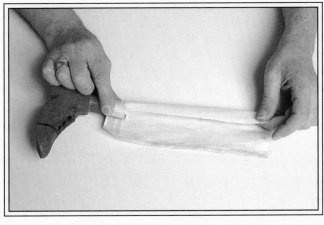

2 *Make the thighs from the same fabric you used to make the lining glove. Glue rectangles of the fabric around the tops of the wooden lower legs to form tubes. Stuff the tubes with scraps of fabric, old stockings or offcuts of foam.*

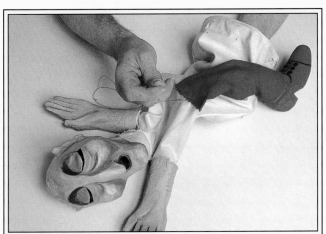

3 *Make pants legs by gluing or stitching the chosen fabric into tube shapes: glue the tops of the pants to the tops of the legs, then stitch the tops of the legs to the glove. Pin them in position first so that you can check the proportions of the puppet's body.*

Now glue or stitch the rest of the costume to the glove, concealing where the legs join the body. When you operate the puppet, the legs swing freely, controlled by the puppet's overall movement.

A Mouth Puppet

Some hand puppets need to be larger than or a different shape from the traditional glove puppet – animals, monsters and Muppet-type characters, for example. Some have very large heads and moving mouths that tend to dominate them. Foam rubber or styrofoam are very popular materials with which to make the head because they are light. The lion illustrated is made from foam rubber.

MAKING THE HEAD

1 Sketch the key features full-face and in profile on the block. Start with a bread knife for the main cuts, add detail with sharp scissors. For a rugged finish, simply pluck pieces of foam from the block.

2 Cut slots in the top jaw to accommodate your fingers and in the bottom jaw for your thumb so that you can open and close the mouth.

3 Join the two halves of the jaw with a hinge made from strong fabric, canvas or soft leather substitute, which is glued in place. If you allow a little space between the jaws at the hinge, you will find that mouth movements can be made more easily.

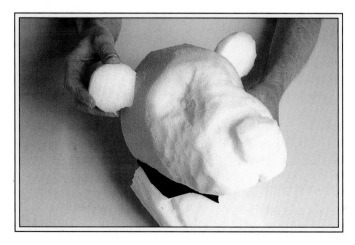

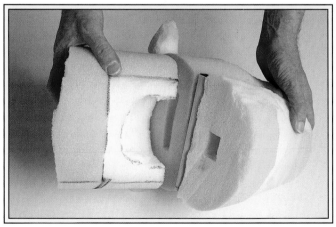

4 Here the hinge has been incorporated in the design of the inside of the mouth. If necessary, line the inside of the mouth with colored felt to hide the hinge. If you are going to cover the entire head with fabric, line the mouth after you have covered the head so that it finishes the edge of the fabric.

5 The back of the head may be made separately and glued on.

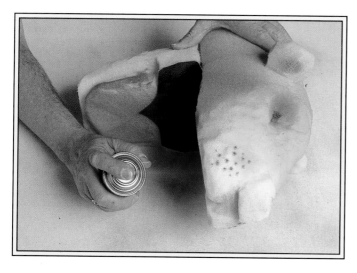

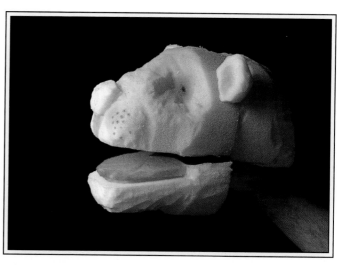

6 *Paint the head or cover with glued-on fabric. Eyes may be sculpted, but for best results carve out the eye sockets. Paint and varnish wooden balls and glue them into the sockets.*

7 *Insert your hand as shown to operate the puppet's mouth.*

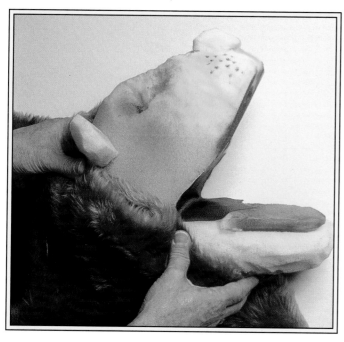

8 *Fabric hangs down from the head, sewn to form the sleeve to cover your operating arm and form the puppet's body. You can line it with sheet foam rubber to give it more shape. The puppet itself does not have arms or hands. Instead, a large costume sleeve is worn by the puppeteer on the spare hand, and this becomes the puppet's hand. Design a loose, long-sleeved glove to accommodate your hand and arm. It is common for this glove to have two or three large fingers and a thumb. Make it from the same material as that covering the puppet. Follow the same stages as those involved in making the standard glove puppet: make a pattern, cut it out of two thicknesses of material (right sides together), sew along the pattern line, trim away the excess fabric, snip close to the stitching between the fingers, then turn the glove right side out.*

When you are performing, keep the costume glove fairly close to the puppet so that they appear to belong together even though they are not actually joined.

Manipulation

GLOVE PUPPETS

The recommended way to operate a glove puppet is to put two fingers (the index and middle finger) inside the neck, two in one arm (the little and ring finger) and the thumb in the other arm. It *looks* rather uncomfortable, but it is not in practice. Do not struggle to separate your fingers sideways; instead, bend the ring and little fingers forward so that they touch your thumb in front of your palm.

This method is recommended because having two fingers inside the neck means that you can create a much greater variety of head movements. To turn the head, for example, you just separate your fingers slightly and wiggle them alternately forward and back. You will see that the head turns independently of the body. To hold any props securely, just hold them between your thumb and the ring and little fingers.

Most people are familiar with ready-made puppets in which the index finger is placed in the neck while the thumb and middle finger work the arms, with the ring and little fingers being held against your palm. This is much less effective and no more comfortable. You can turn the head only by turning your whole hand and, therefore, the whole puppet. Handling of props is no better – in fact, there is a tendency for the two spare fingers to make this more difficult. Also, if you relax these fingers, they drift out to the front of the glove, creating an unsightly bulge.

MOUTH PUPPETS

With mouth puppets it is important to remember that the audience is usually lower than the puppets, so you must make a conscious effort to allow for this. Keep your wrist bent forward so that the puppet relates to the audience; otherwise, the puppet will appear to be staring into space.

ALL PUPPETS

Practice is necessary if you are to make your puppet's movements look convincing. Try walking the puppet, bowing, pointing; make it look happy, sad, thoughtful, surprised, furtive, afraid, angry. Can you distinguish the emotions? What characterizes the differences? Observe people – this will help you to understand movement and improve your performance.

3

Rod
Puppets

—

A Simple Rod Puppet

The rod puppet is built on a central rod attached to the head. This puppet is sculpted from styrofoam and covered with white glue and paper.

MAKING THE HEAD

1 *Establish the basic shape with a hand saw, a hacksaw blade or a bread knife.*

2 *Carve finer details with a sharp craft knife or a rasp or pluck pieces out by hand. Make a hole up into the head with a rasp* *or screwdriver blade. Insert and glue into the head a dowel rod of up to 1in (25mm) diameter.*

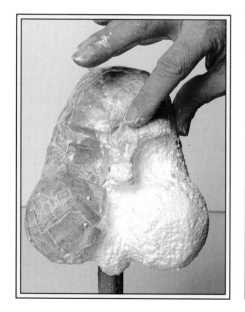

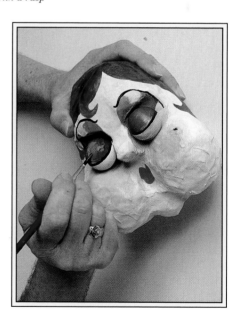

3 *Use white or carpenter's pearl glue to cover the styrofoam with at least three layers of paper torn into small pieces. Using different colored papers for alternate layers helps to guarantee full coverage. Allow each layer to dry before you apply the next.*

4 *Apply a coat of glue to the final layer of paper. When it is dry, sand it lightly, and apply a coat of white latex paint.*

5 *When this has dried, paint and finish the head as appropriate to its character.*

MAKING THE BODY

1 Cut a shoulder block from a piece of foam rubber and shape it using sharp scissors. Make a hole down through the center of the block to accommodate the rod.

2 If you do not wish the head to turn, insert the rod and glue to the foam. If you do want the head to turn, make sure the hole in the block is large enough to allow it to turn smoothly on the rod without wobbling. Then follow the next three stages.

3 Cut two large washer shapes from the bases or lids of plastic cartons.

4 Thread them onto the rod, one above and one below the shoulder block to prevent the neck and shoulder block from clinging and so hindering the turning.

5 Beneath the lower washer, glue a collar of foam rubber to the rod. This secures the shoulders, but allows the rod to turn freely.

MAKING THE ARMS AND HANDS

The arms are made from a length of rope, which is firm but also possesses just the right amount of flexibility for realistic movements. The hands are cut from foam rubber.

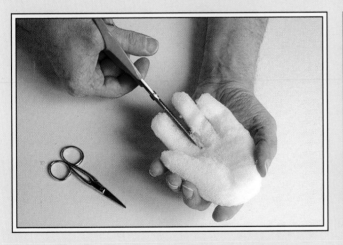

1 Establish the basic outline of the hands, then refine the shape with small scissors, snipping a little at a time.

2 With a sharp knife, make a slit along the top of the shoulder block and spread glue along the slit and insert the rope into it, letting suitable lengths of rope hang down each side.

3 Cut a slot from the palm to the heel of each hand to accommodate the ends of the rope arms and glue the rope securely in place.

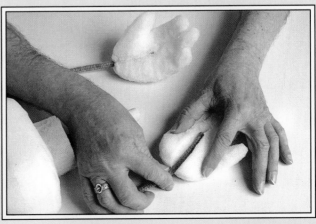

TIPS FOR THE CONTROL ROD

A long control rod allows the puppet to be held high and to be any size, but be careful about its weight because it might become difficult to control. A long rod also limits body movement as the puppet cannot bend at the waist. With a short control rod, your wrist is effectively the puppet's waist, so its range of movements is then enhanced considerably. Ideally, its length should be such that, when assembled, it reaches to approximately 3in. (7.5cm) above the puppet's waist.

DRESSING THE PUPPET

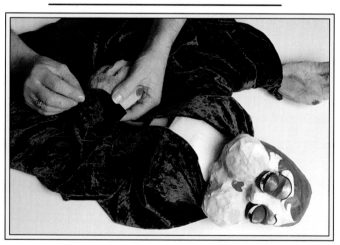

The costume is a flowing robe made from pieces of material that are suitably gathered and draped.

MAKING THE HAND CONTROLS

Make the hand controls from lengths of 12 gauge galvanized wire (coathanger wire). Straighten the wire and cut a length that is sufficient to permit you to operate the hands without your own hands being seen by the audience.

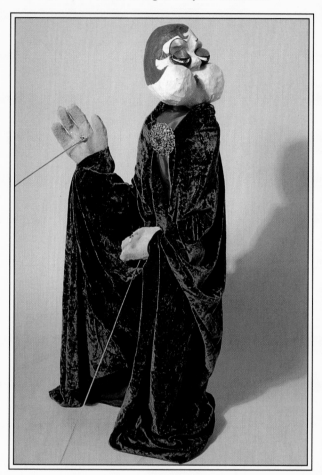

1 Make a loop at the top of the wire and seal the closure with clear contact glue.

2 Attach the wire to the palm of the hand with strong thread (Dacron braided nylon fishing line is ideal). Do this by tying the thread to a clear or hand-colored button and passing the thread through the loop in the wire.

3 Use a large-eyed sewing needle to stitch the thread to the hand, making sure it goes through the rope inside the hand. Wind the thread around between the button and the cord a few times before finally securing it. Make it tight enough to give clean and direct control over the hand movement, but not so tight that the wire is prevented from pivoting smoothly on the thread.

OPERATING YOUR ROD PUPPET

Head control is effected by holding and turning the head rod with one hand. At the same time, operate one or two hand wires with your other hand (described on page 56). When you turn the head, you will find that the body stays in the same position, partly because of the weight of the costume and partly because of the control you have over it through the hand rods.

A Rod Puppet with a Nodding Head

This head is sculpted from styrofoam and covered with white glue and paper. Establish the shape using a saw, bread knife or rasp. Carve the finer details with a sharp knife.

The central control rod is made from a length of approximately ¾-in. (18-mm) diameter dowel. The head pivots on the rod, which is held in place by a piece of wire.

1 Cut an elongated hole up into the head, making it wide enough to accommodate the central control rod.

2 Secure the control rod in a vice and, with a fine gouge, chisel or craft knife, carefully cut a groove along the rear of the rod. This is for the control wire to be added later.

3 Drill across the top of the control rod a hole large enough for a piece of strong galvanized wire to thread through and turn freely. Cut the wire a little wider than the head.

NOTE

Push the wire into one side of the head, through the head, through the control rod and out the other side. Do not secure the pivot wire until the nodding control mechanism has been completed and the shoulders are attached. So that the rod does not move sideways, cut two pieces of dowel to act as spacers between the rod and the head. Drill a hole for the wire through the length of each dowel. Assemble the parts with the dowels on each side of the rod.

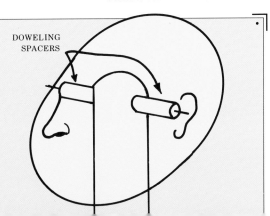

DOWELING SPACERS

THE NODDING MECHANISM

The nodding mechanism moves the head smoothly and holds it in any position you want. It works by means of a strong galvanized wire (coathanger wire) lever that runs up the back of the control rod (in the groove cut earlier) from a thumb rest and is secured in the back of the head.

1 *Secure the wire to the rod with small staples, but make sure that the wire can move freely up and down. The top and bottom staples set the limits to the movement of the wire.*

2 *Angle the top of the wire making the end into an elongated loop. Use a piece of galvanized wire to link the loop to the head in the same way as, and parallel with, the pivot wire. Get the mechanism working smoothly as shown before securing it in the head.*

Attach the shoulder block (see opposite) before stage 3.

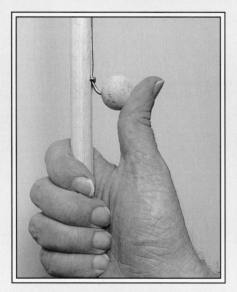

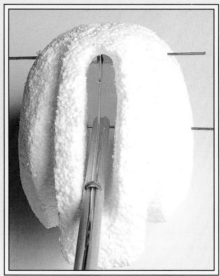

3 *Bend the bottom end of the control wire outward and glue onto it a wooden ball with a hole pre-drilled in it. Move the wire up and down to effect nodding movement; some adjustment to the angle of the control wire may be necessary to achieve smooth movement.*

4 *When the nodding mechanism is complete and working smoothly, glue the pivot wire and the loop-link wire in the head, with dowel spacers used as before to stop the control wire from moving sideways. Cut the pivot wire and loop-link wire to the width of the head.*

MAKING THE SHOULDERS

The shoulder block is attached before stage 3 of the nodding control mechanism is completed. Make the shoulder block from plywood padded with foam rubber. It is secured to the central rod with cord, which holds it in place without being rigid.

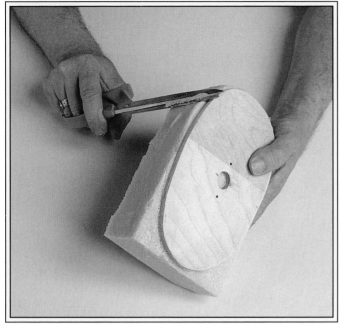

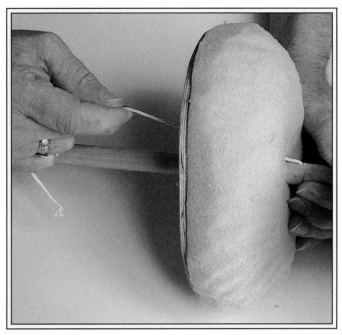

1 Cut the plywood to shape with a jigsaw or coping saw. Drill a hole down through the center for the control rod. Then glue a block of foam rubber to the plywood and trim to shape.

2 Drill a hole across the control rod and another two holes down through the shoulders as shown. Thread cord through the rod and down through the holes in the shoulder block. Knot the ends and seal the knots with clear contact glue.

MAKING THE HANDS AND ARMS

The hands are shaped from foam rubber as described previously.

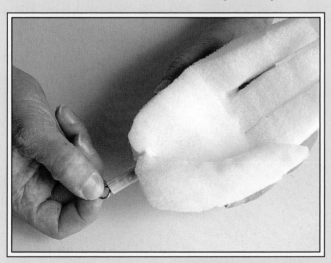

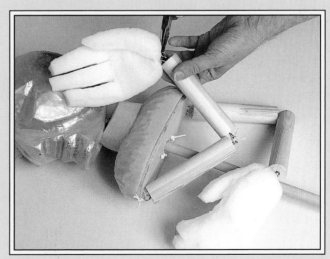

1 A piece of dowel with a screw-eye in one end is glued into a hole made in the heel of the hand. The arms are joined to the shoulders in a similar way using a length of cord. The arms are made from dowel rods with screw-eyes and cords for elbow and wrist joints.

2 Drill holes through the ends of the shoulders. Thread cord through the holes and tie it to screw-eyes screwed into the tops of the arms.

The puppet appears at waist height and has neither legs nor feet.

Cover the styrofoam with white glue and small pieces of paper, finishing with a coat of glue. When it is dry, sand lightly and coat with white latex paint.

Paint the puppet's head and hands.

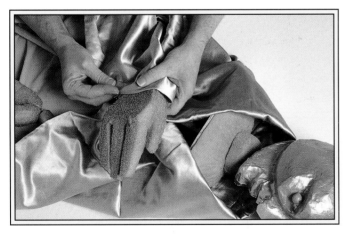

Dress the puppet with draped fabric or a sewn or glued costume, assembling it directly on the puppet itself.

MAKING HAND CONTROLS

Hand wires are made from galvanized wire (coathanger wire) with loops in one end and dowel handles at the other as described previously. Attach the loops in the wires to the palms of the hands with strong thread sewn through the hand and around the dowels inside the foam rubber.

Again, the main rod and head action are controlled with one hand and the hand wires operated by your free hand.

A Puppet with Turning Head Control

MAKING THE HEAD

You can make the head using one of the techniques given in the Introduction, but the plaster filler and cheesecloth technique is suitable for making the head illustrated here.

This puppet has direct head-turning control. You will need a central rod, made from approximately ¾-in (18-mm) diameter dowel and a piece of tubing that fits snugly over the rod, but allows it to turn freely inside. (A piece of plastic plumbing pipe that is ¾in. (18mm) across the internal diameter is ideal, but you can also use aluminum or strong cardboard tubing.)

THE PLASTER FILLER AND CHEESECLOTH TECHNIQUE

1 *Make a clay model of the head on a modeling stand, then cover it with a layer of squares of dampened tissue paper.*

2 *Apply three layers of small squares of cheesecloth dipped in plaster filler, pressing each layer well onto the previous one. Use absorbent cotton dipped in the plaster filler for the detailed areas.*

3 *When the plaster has dried, carefully cut open the head and remove the clay mold. Rejoin the two plaster halves of the head with glue, then apply a final layer of plaster filler and cheesecloth.*

4 *When the head has dried completely, refine the shape with a craft knife if necessary and lightly sand the surface smooth. Paint and finish the head.*

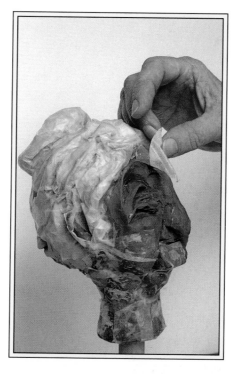
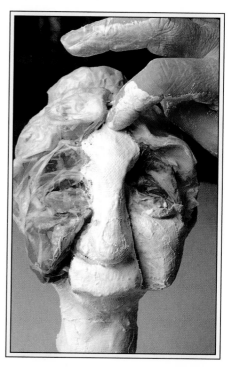
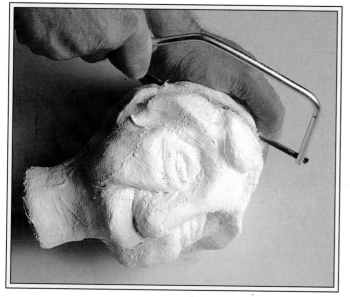
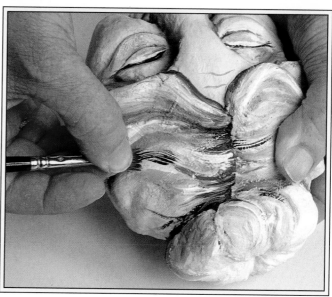

MAKING THE SHOULDERS

Make a shoulder block from a piece of foam rubber.

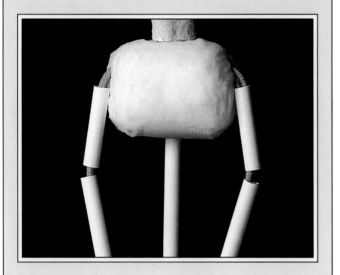

1 *Make a hole in the center of the foam rubber block. Then glue it to the top of the central control tube.*

2 *Trim the block to shape. If you wish, you can make a complete torso in foam rubber.*

MAKING THE ARMS

The arms are made from rope. Here plastic tubing has been used to give them more bulk, but you could also use foam rubber.

1 *Cut a length of rope, nearly double the length of the required arm span, and glue it into a slot in the shoulder block, as described for the simple rod puppet.*

2 *Loop the rope at the wrist and bind the double length together with thread. Slip two pieces of plastic plumbing pipe over each rope arm and secure them in position with small pieces of foam rubber glued into the ends.*

MAKING THE HANDS

The hands are made from foam rubber as they are quite large.

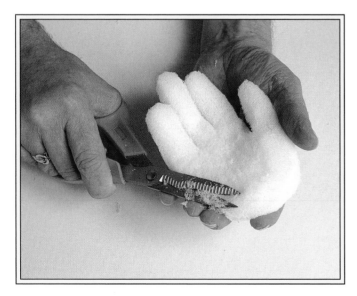

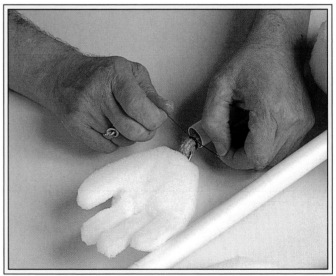

1 *Cut out the shape with sharp scissors.*

2 *Bend a piece of galvanized wire (coathanger wire) into a U-shape and link it through the loop in the rope at the wrists. Then glue the ends of the wire securely into the heel of the hand to effect the wrist joint.*

Paint the hands, applying the paint with your fingertips so that it does not soak into the foam.

ATTACHING THE HEAD TO THE CONTROL ROD

1 Glue the central control rod into the head and hold it firmly in place with pieces of foam rubber glued and inserted around the top of the rod and the bottom of the neck.

2 Secure further with a screw through the top of the head if necessary. Insert the head rod into the main control tube.

DRESSING THE PUPPET

Stitch or glue the costume to the puppet before adding the hand controls.

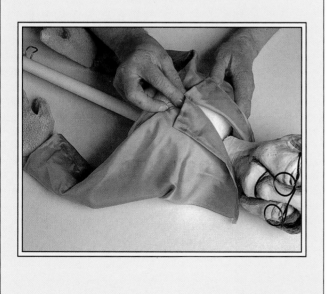

MAKING THE HEAD CONTROL

The head control is reasonably straightforward to put together and is worthwhile because it gives more direct control over the turning movement.

1 Mark on the back of the tube the point where your thumb will rest when you are holding it for working the puppet. At this point, saw two parallel slots across the tube, approximately ¼in (4mm) apart. Cut out the piece of tube between these slots and smooth the sawn edges.

2 Insert the fitted head rod fully into the tube, leaving a small space between the neck and the shoulder block. (If they stick together, insert two plastic washers, cut from plastic cartons, below the neck.) Position the head of the puppet so that it is facing straight ahead, then, on the rod, mark the position of the slot you made in the tube.

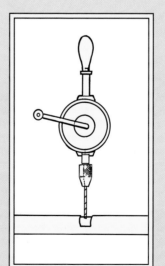
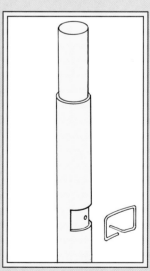

3 Remove the rod from the tube and drill a hole in the rod in the center of the slot marking. Put the rod back in the tube.

4 Bend a length of 12 gauge galvanized wire (coathanger wire) into the shape shown to make a thumb rest. Glue the end of the wire into the hole in the dowel.

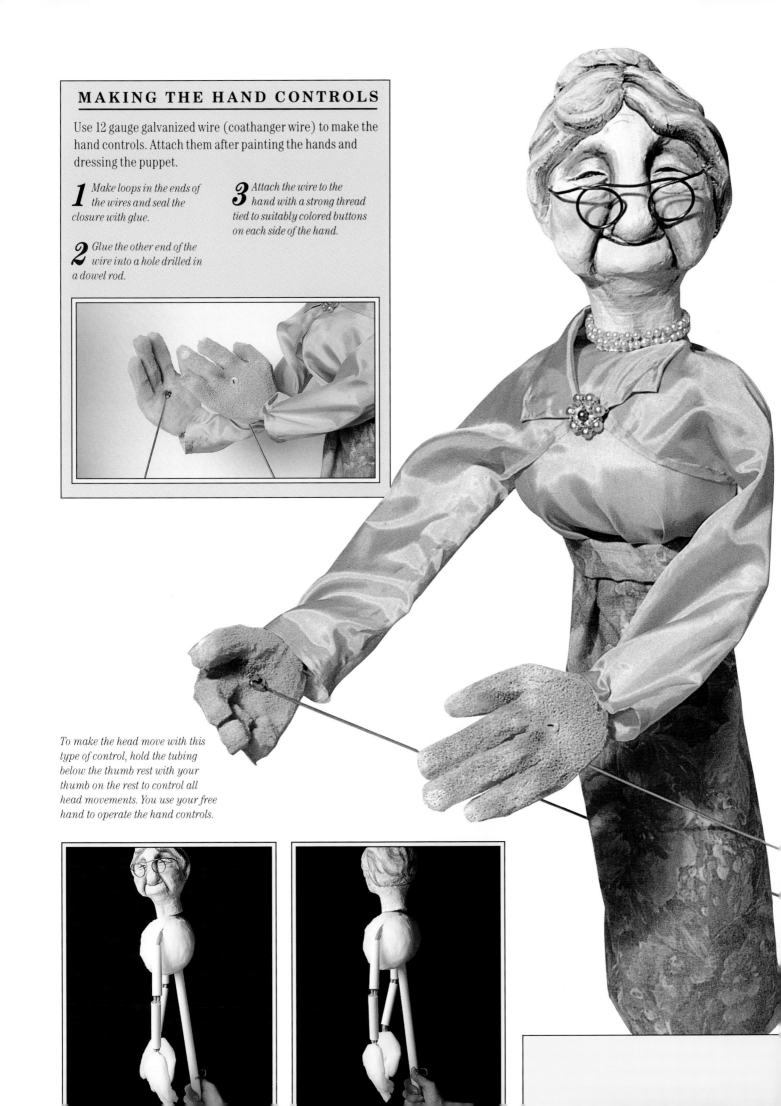

MAKING THE HAND CONTROLS

Use 12 gauge galvanized wire (coathanger wire) to make the hand controls. Attach them after painting the hands and dressing the puppet.

1 Make loops in the ends of the wires and seal the closure with glue.

2 Glue the other end of the wire into a hole drilled in a dowel rod.

3 Attach the wire to the hand with a strong thread tied to suitably colored buttons on each side of the hand.

To make the head move with this type of control, hold the tubing below the thumb rest with your thumb on the rest to control all head movements. You use your free hand to operate the hand controls.

A Rod Puppet with Nodding and Turning Head Control

This puppet has a fully articulated head, which is achieved by a single control wire operated by your thumb. Plastic wood has been used for this puppet.

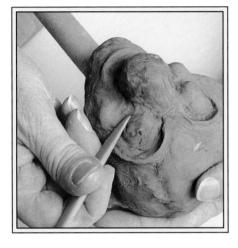

1 Build the head in clay on a modeling stand. As it is to nod, it is made without a neck.

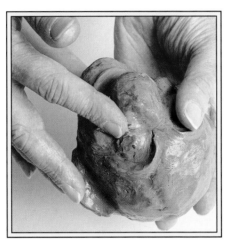

2 Cover the clay head with petroleum jelly to prevent the plastic wood from sticking to it.

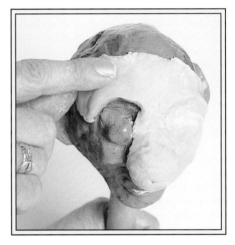

3 Cover the head with plastic wood about ⅛ in. (3mm) thick, applied in small pieces. Dip it in acetone to help blend the pieces together. Work details with modeling tools or a fine craft knife.

4 When the plastic wood is thoroughly dry – after at least 24 hours and possibly longer – cut open the head with a craft knife or junior hacksaw. Follow a line over the top of the head and down behind the ears, with a V-cut on top to facilitate accurate rejoining of the shells. Cut through the clay with strong thread or fine wire (in the manner of cutting cheese).

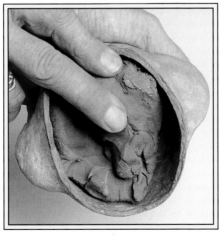

5 Carefully scoop the clay from the shell. Hold the shells up to the light to identify any weak points that may need strengthening. Before applying plastic wood inside the shell, scrape away any clay or grease and smear with glue. (For other puppets requiring internal dowel rods, they would be inserted at this stage and secured with glue and more plastic wood.)

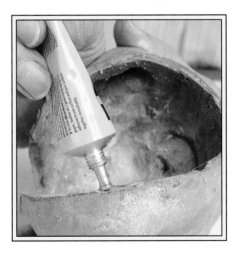

6 Rejoin the shells with glue and cover the joint with plastic wood. If your modeling is not strong enough, you can reinforce it with more plastic wood at this stage. With a coarse rasp, make an elongated hole in the base of the head to permit nodding movement on the control rod.

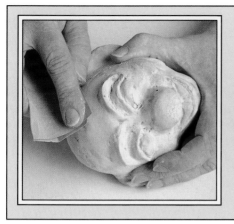

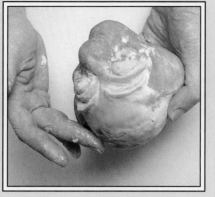

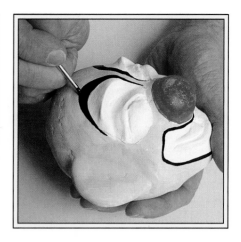

7 When it is dry, sand the head. For a very smooth finish, apply a fine film of plastic wood to the head and smooth acetone over the surface with your fingers. You can achieve a surface smooth enough not to need further sanding.

8 Paint and finish in keeping with the character.

Make the shoulder block from foam rubber trimmed to shape, and glue it to a central control tube (plastic plumbing tube). Leave enough tube above the shoulders to fit inside the head.

THE HEAD CONTROL
The control mechanism is similar to that described for the rod puppet with a nodding head.

1 Attach the head to a grooved control rod and to a galvanized wire (coathanger wire) lever with an elongated loop in the end.

2 Find the spot on the tube where it is most comfortable for you to rest your thumb as if you were operating the puppet, and cut out a rectangle that is large enough to permit movement of the control wire in all directions. The size of this window depends on the distance the wire must move, but, as a guide, this one is 2in. (5cm) high and its width is halfway around the tube.

3 Cut a second horizontal slot near the bottom of the tube.

4 Insert the central rod into the tube and mark the position of the window on the rod. Remove the rod and, in the center of the mark, cut a slot to take the control wire (to do this, drill a series of small holes and clean out the remaining excess wood with a knife or file).

5 Replace the rod and control wire, fitting the wire through the window. Bend the wire to form a thumb rest with a short end projecting into the vertical slot in the rod.

6 To ensure that the rod just moves horizontally, not vertically, screw a round-headed screw with a washer threaded onto it through the small slot in the tube. Do not overtighten the screw.

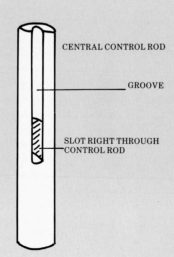

CENTRAL CONTROL ROD

GROOVE

SLOT RIGHT THROUGH CONTROL ROD

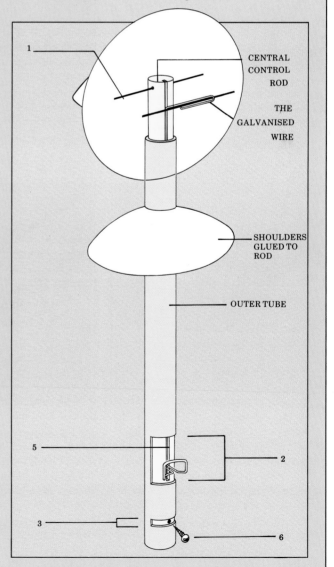

1

CENTRAL CONTROL ROD

THE GALVANISED WIRE

SHOULDERS GLUED TO ROD

OUTER TUBE

5

2

3

6

Hold the central control rod and move the thumb rest left or right to turn the head, or up and down to make the puppet look up and down.

MAKING THE HANDS AND ARMS

The hands are made from blocks of wood, held in a vice and shaped with a saw, chisels and/or rasps. This puppet has a very basic hand shape with detail painted on.

The arms are made from dowel with elbow and wrist joints created by interlocked screw-eyes. Cut away the dowels at the elbows to allow them to bend. The arms are joined to the body by screw-eyes and cord: a piece of cord attached to both arms is glued into a slot cut across the top of the shoulder block.

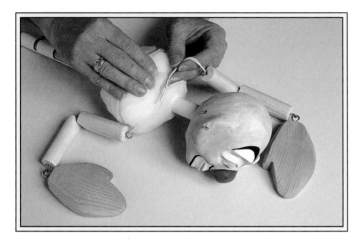

Dress the puppet before attaching hand controls.

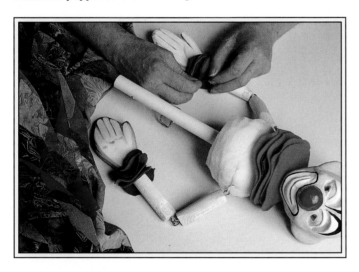

MAKING THE CONTROL WIRES

Hand wires are made from galvanized wire (coathanger wire) with loops in one end as described previously.

1 Drill a series of holes to create a slot in the side of each hand.

2 Insert the hand wire loop into the slot and secure it with a small nail through the palm. This allows the wire to pivot and enables direct and controlled manipulation. Again, the main rod and head action are controlled with one hand, while the hand wires are operated by your free hand.

You can achieve a good deal of movement through the central control rod, but the overall expression of the puppet depends a good deal on the movements of the hands and arms. The movements need to be positive and deliberate, not jerky or rushed. The puppets should move cleanly from one gesture or position to the next, and do not be afraid to hold a pose before moving to the next.

When you first try a rod puppet, it is often easiest to hold it with one hand, using the other hand to operate one puppet hand at a time. This also happens to be a convenient way to make particular gestures, but it is not good technique to stick to this method all the time. You will find that if you start off with this method, you will soon be able to add to the range of movements you can make the puppet do. As you get more proficient, you can progress to the recommended method, which is to hold the central rod with one hand and both hand wires with the other. It needs a little practice, but you will soon find that this is a lot easier than it looks.

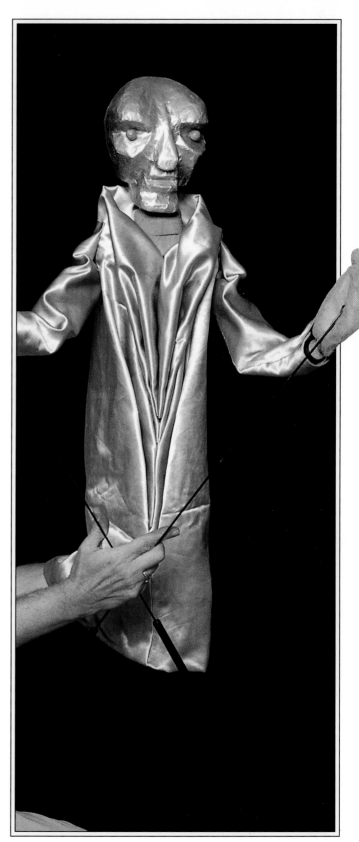

You will find that you can achieve a good deal of control by:

● holding the two hand controls close together
● holding the hand control handles together, but keeping the wires in a *slight* V shape by holding a finger between them
● holding the wires in a *wide* V shape by hooking your thumb and index finger between the wires and spreading them apart as shown.

When you need to use your free hand to move a single hand control, it is sometimes helpful to support the other hand control with the little finger of your other hand. This often looks better because the puppet's hand is not hanging limp by its side.

4

Marionettes

—

A Simple Marionette

For a simple marionette, make the head and neck in one piece using one of the techniques outlined in the Introduction. The puppet described here uses the paste and paper method, the key stages of which are given below.

MAKING THE HEAD

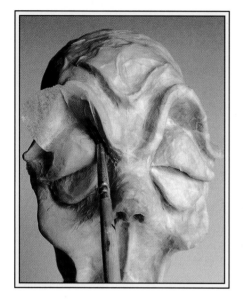

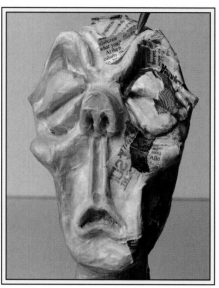

1 *Sculpt the basic head in clay on a modeling stand. Normally you should insert cardboard ears into the model (see page 30), but this puppet has been designed without visible ears. Cover the head with squares of dampened tissue paper.*

2 *Apply at least four layers of overlapping squares of newspaper using white glue or cellular paste, working any detailed areas with tissue paper.*

3 *Finish with a coat of glue. Here a coat of latex paint has also been applied.*

4 *When the paper has dried, cut open the head and carefully remove the clay mold.*

5 *If the ears are not strong enough to attach the head string to, cut a piece of ³⁄₈-in (9-mm) diameter dowel to fit inside the head between the ears, as in this example. Glue the dowel across the head at a point that will enable the strings to it to hold the head in the required position. Insert small screw-eyes through the head shell and into the ends of the dowel, for attaching the head strings later.*

6 *Rejoin the head with glue, aligning them carefully, and cover the joint with another layer of white glue or cellular paste and paper. At the same time, glue into the neck cavity a piece of dowel that is the same diameter as the inside of the neck and attach a screw-eye to the lower end. Glue three layers of paper over the bottom of this neck and over the end of the dowel to help to secure it very firmly.*

MAKING THE BODY

The body is constructed on a central synthetic leather or fabric base that also serves as the waist and hip joints.

1 *Shape blocks of balsa wood with a saw, rasp and craft knife to create the upper body and pelvis.*

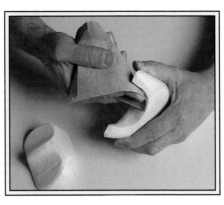

2 *Cut away the top of the body to accommodate the neck.*

3 *Cut a strip of synthetic leather or canvas to the shape of the body, leaving enough spare to make the hip joints.*

4 *Glue the body shapes to the central fabric.*

5 *Hold the neck in place and push a piece of galvanized wire (coathanger wire) through the top of the upper body and the screw-eye in the neck to form the neck joint. Bend the ends of the wire into loops for arm joints.*

6 *Drill two holes at the shoulder blade level and glue dowel pegs into them with woodworking glue, first putting small screw-eyes into the ends, to which you will attach shoulder strings later. In the same way insert another peg with a screw-eye in the end into the rear of the pelvis. This is for attaching a back string.*

MAKING THE HANDS

Make the hands from blocks of wood.

1 *Place the wood in a vice and sculpt the basic shape, using rasps. (It helps to leave some wood that is extra to the desired shape at the wrist so that it can be held in the vice.)*

2 *Add detail using a chisel, craft knife and files. These hands have been designed simply, with grooves to indicate the fingers, and a little shaping of the thumbs. Cut away*

any excess wood left at the heel of the hand and sand the hand smooth. Fit a screw-eye into the heel of each hand.

MAKING THE ARMS

The lower arms are made from lengths of dowel and the upper arms from cord.

1 *Fit screw-eyes in each end of the dowel. Make the wrist joint with interlocking screw-eyes.*

2 *To the screw-eye at the elbow, attach a piece of cord to form the upper arm, and tie it to the wire loop on the body. If you wish, you can pad the cord with foam rubber to give the arm more bulk.*

MAKING THE LEGS AND FEET

The legs are made from four blocks of balsa wood and have strap joints for knees.
The feet are made from blocks of balsa wood, using the same techniques that you used to make the hands and body.

1 *With a junior hacksaw, cut slots into the ends of each leg section (widthwise at the hips and knees, and from front go back at the ankles). Make all the slots very fine, except at the ankle which should be a little more than the thickness of a screw-eye.*

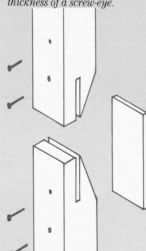

2 *Cut wedge-shaped pieces from the backs of the knees so that the finished legs will be able to bend.*

3 *Glue strips of the joining material into the slots cut at the knees; the material should be wide enough to hold at the sides while securing it. Make sure that the leg parts meet at the front of the knees to prevent double-jointed knees. Secure all the strap joints with small nails, putting a spot of glue over the heads of the nails to secure them. Trim away the spare material at the edges.*

1 *Put a suitably sized block of balsa wood in a vice and shape it with a rasp, using small files to add details, and then sand it smooth. Drill down into each foot at the ankle a hole into which you glue a piece of dowel with a screw-eye in the top.*

2 *Place the feet so that the screw-eyes fit into the slots in the ankles. Secure the screw-eyes by drilling a guide hole and then gently tapping a round nail of suitable length through the side of each ankle. The nail passes just under the*

inside of the top of each screw-eye. Make sure that there is enough space between the foot and leg for there to be a little flexibility, but not so much that the toe will drag as the puppet walks. Secure the nail with a spot of glue.

3 *To make the hip joints, glue into the tops of the thighs the material that is attached to the central body. Make sure there is enough space to permit movement. Secure the straps with small nails and add a spot of glue to the heads. Trim away the excess at the edges.*

PAINTING AND FINISHING THE PUPPET

Paint and finish the head and hands at the same time to match skin tones. For this puppet a wig has been created from cord: some has been plaited and some wound around, and glued to, small bunches of drinking straws. You might need to invent methods of securing the parts while they are drying. In this case a plastic bag was used rather like a hairnet.

Before stringing the puppet, add the costume.

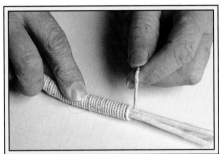
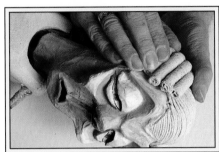

MAKING AN AIRPLANE CONTROL

Marionette manipulation is easier than most people think although, as with all puppets, you need to practice to achieve convincing movement. Most of the strings support the puppet, so you can make the puppet move in all sorts of ways just by tilting and turning the main control. It is therefore a mistake to make the control too simple, as this will make manipulation more difficult – you will have to pull individual strings for the same effect.

The standard airplane control consists of a main bar of 8 × 1 × 1in (20 × 2.5 × 2.5cm) wood from which are suspended dowel head and shoulder bars and a removable hand bar; a leg bar is secured to the control, forming a T-shape. All dowels are ⅜in (9mm) in diameter.

Normally holes are drilled through the control in order to attach the strings. This is preferable to attaching screw-eyes, which tend to catch in the strings of other puppets.

1 *Drill three holes down through the main bar: one small hole near the back to take the back string, two slightly larger holes for cords – one for the shoulder bar a little in front of the first hole, the other for the head bar, forward of the mid-point of the main control bar.*

2 *Cut two dowels to use as the head and shoulder bars. Make them a little wider than the parts to which their strings are to be attached. Carefully drill a hole down through the mid-point of each bar for the cord to join it to the main control. Drill small holes for the head and shoulder strings near the ends of each bar.*

3 *Cut a dowel leg bar about 8in (20cm) long. About 1in (2.5cm) from the front of the main control bar drill a horizontal hole to accommodate the leg bar (it should be a secure fit). Drill holes for the leg strings through the ends of the leg bar, then glue it in place.*

4 *Attach the head bar to the main control by threading a cord down through both pieces and knotting each end of the cord. Seal the knots with clear contact glue. Attach the shoulder bar to the main control in the same way.*

5 *Drill holes for the strings through the ends of a dowel for the hand bar. Attach a screw-eye to the center of the hand bar and a hook into the front end of the control. Suspend the hand bar from this hook.*

6 *With the edge of a file, make a groove around each bar where the thread is to be attached. These will help you when you are securing the threads.*

7 *Sand the whole control smooth as any roughness will fray the strings.*

HOOK FOR HANGING UP STRINGED PUPPET

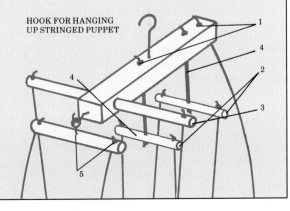

STRINGING THE MARIONETTE

Use strong black or green thread – for example, Dacron braided nylon fishing line, strength 10lb. Wax the thread with beeswax before using it and periodically afterward to strengthen it and prevent it from fraying and tangling. Use a needle to stitch the thread through the costume and the screw-eyes inside (do not attach the strings to the costume alone).

1 *Attach the head strings so that the puppet will stand on the stage when the control is held at elbow height.*

2 *Attach the shoulder strings and adjust the tension so that the head sits at the required angle to the body.*

3 *Attach the back string, keeping it slightly slack so that it does not impede the puppet's movements.*

4 *To attach the hand strings, drill a small hole through the hand to pass the thread through and knot the end (attach the thread to the part of the hand that will enable it to be held in the required position). The thread should be just long enough to allow you to unhook the hand bar without moving the hands.*

5 *Attach the leg strings to the leg bar and to the knees by threading a large needle and pushing it through the balsa legs, back through a new hole and knotting it at the front of the knee. Seal all the knots with clear glue and trim the loose ends.*

OPERATING THE AIRPLANE CONTROL

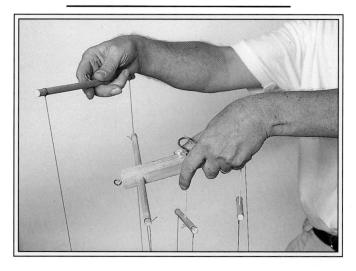

Hold the main control in one hand and tilt it forward to make the puppet nod (with your free hand you can raise the shoulder bar).

To turn the head, tilt the main control very slightly to take the weight on the shoulder bar, then turn the head bar with your free hand.

To make the puppet bow, lower the control forward, at the same time taking the weight on the back string.

To make the puppet walk, rock or paddle the main control.

To lower the puppet to one knee, lower the control while also lifting one leg string forward with your free hand.

To manipulate the hands, unhook and move the hand control rod. Often, though, you will find that it is best to operate the strings themselves with your free hand.

A Standard Marionette

MAKING THE HEAD

The head of this puppet is made from plastic wood. The techniques for modeling using this material are described in detail on pages 53–54, but the following will remind you of the main steps.

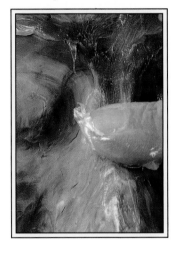

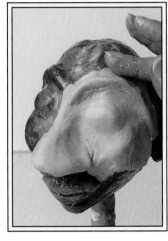

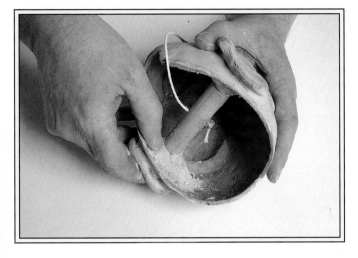

1 Make the head without a neck, which will be made from wood. Sculpt the head in clay on a modeling stand and press cardboard ears into the clay. Smear petroleum jelly over the head before applying the plastic wood.

2 Cover the head with an ⅛-in (3-mm) thick layer of plastic wood, applied in small pieces, and use acetone to help you blend the pieces together. Smear the cardboard ears with glue before covering them with the plastic wood. Model the details using a modeling tool or craft knife.

3 When the head is completely dry (this will take at least 24 hours), cut it open using a craft knife or small saw. Carefully scoop the clay out from the shells. Strengthen any weak points by applying more plastic wood, but remember to scrape away any remaining clay or grease and smear the area with glue when applying pieces to the inside. Cut a piece of ⅜-in (9-mm) diameter dowel to fit between the ears inside the front half of the head. Drill a small hole through the mid-point of the dowel and thread an 8-in (20-cm) length of strong cord through the hole. Knot one end of the cord and secure the knot with clear contact glue. Scrape clean the points where the dowel makes contact with the inside of the head and fix the dowel securely in place, using both glue and plastic wood. Make sure that the knot is facing the top of the head.

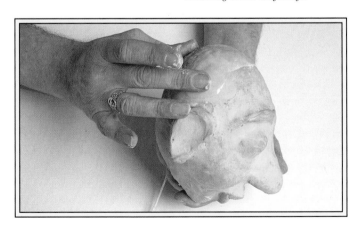

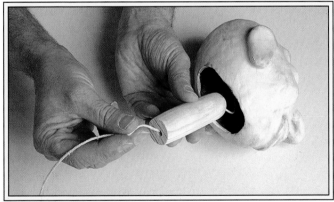

4 Rejoin the head using clear contact glue. Cover the joint smoothly with plastic wood. (Remember to use acetone to thin plastic wood for a finishing layer; when it is dry, finely sand it smooth and repeat the process for a very smooth finish.)

5 Use a rasp to shape a neck from a suitably sized piece of dowel or block of wood, tapering toward each end. Drill a hole through the length of the dowel. If you do not have a long drill bit, you will need to drill very carefully from both ends toward the center and jiggle with your drill until the holes align. Thread through the neck the cord attached to the dowel in the head.

Paint the head and neck with undercoat before proceeding so that they can be drying while you make the body.

MAKING THE BODY

Now construct the body. This method is an alternative to that given for the simple marionette.

1 Use a coping saw to cut the upper body from a sheet of plywood. Drill four holes through it, as shown, for the arm, neck and waist joints.

2 Tie and glue the neck cord to the neck hole in the plywood. You might find it helpful to insert a wooden ball between the neck and upper body to improve movement.

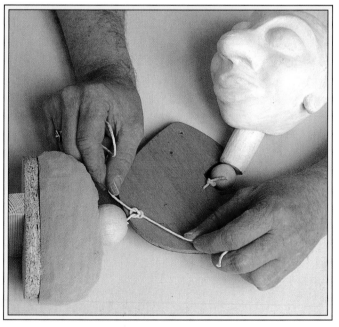

3 Make the pelvis from two pieces of wood, suitably shaped and glued and screwed together. Insert a screw-eye in the middle at the top and pad the shape by gluing foam rubber to the wood.

4 Drill a hole through a large wooden ball and attach the pelvis to the upper body with cord threaded through the ball (this improves the waist movement). The pelvis might appear to twist unrestricted, but this will not happen when the costume and leg strings are attached. Insert a small screw-eye in the back of the pelvis for attaching the back string later. Glue foam rubber to each side of the plywood upper body piece and trim it to shape. Make two holes in the foam rubber back. Glue dowel pegs into them after fixing small screw-eyes to which the shoulder strings will be attached later.

MAKING THE ARMS

Make arms from blocks of wood or lengths of softwood dowel. Do not, however, use thin dowel because this does not have the necessary bulk or strength for arms. Here wooden blocks have been used and shaved as necessary with a rasp and a chisel.

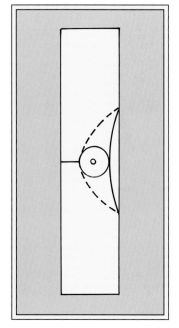

1 Make the elbow joint by cutting an open mortise-and-tenon joint. Design the joint and draw the required shapes onto blocks of wood.

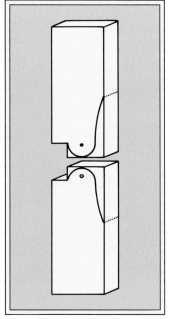

2 Place the pieces in a woodworking vice and, with a saw, remove the areas shown in the diagram.

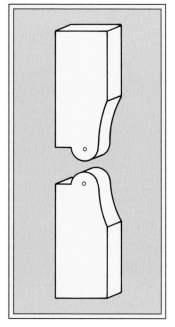

3 Using a rasp or file, round the corners on the parts that overlap and then finish the

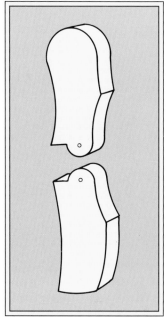

shaping of the arms: remember to shape them also to fit well against the body.

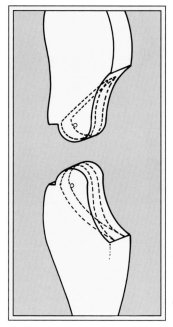

4 In the ends of each section make two saw cuts (those shown as dotted lines in the diagram).

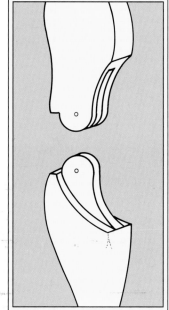

5 Using a saw, craft knife or narrow chisel, remove the wood in the center of the upper arms, leaving a slot. Similarly, remove the wood on the outsides of the lower arms, leaving the section in the middle intact. Sand all surfaces smooth.

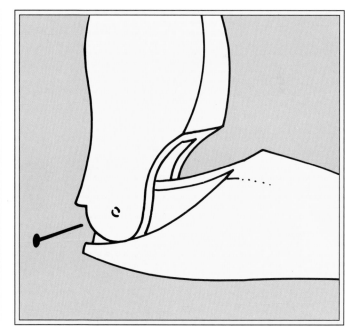

6 Position the elbow sections together as you want them to sit, then drill a small hole through the center of the overlapping parts. Separate the parts and enlarge the hole in the center section slightly so that it will move when a nail is inserted. Reassemble the joint and insert the nail. When the joint is working smoothly, seal the ends of the nail with a spot of glue.

The arms could be made using a strap joint, described on page 60.

MAKING THE HANDS

Plastic wood hands are excellent for this puppet. Once you have established the basic shape, you can carve, file or sand it or build it up with more plastic wood.

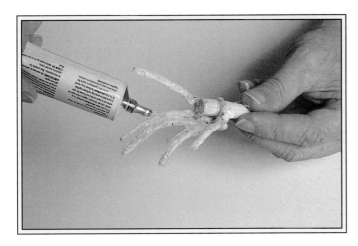

1 *Intertwine pipe cleaners and bend them until you have the basic positions of the fingers and thumb. Glue a short piece of dowel into the palm of each hand as shown so that you can make strong wrist joints later.*

2 *Cover the pipe cleaners and dowel with a clear contact glue and then press on the plastic wood, in fairly large pieces. Do not try to attach it to individual fingers, but instead make a larger pad.*

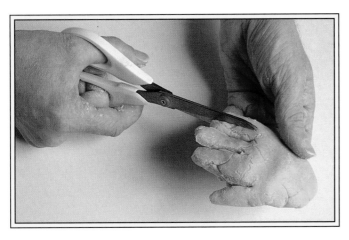

3 *Snip between the fingers with a pair of scissors. Shape the fingers using acetone to soften the plastic wood as necessary. When it has hardened, build up or cut away the plastic wood and finish as described earlier for the head.*

4 *Insert a screw-eye into the dowel at the heel of the hand. Carefully drill a hole in the end of each arm (the wrist end) in which to insert the loop of the screw-eye fixed in the hand. Then drill a small hole across the wrist through the loop. Insert a nail into this hole to secure the screw-eye and effect the wrist joint. Add a spot of glue to the head of the nail.*

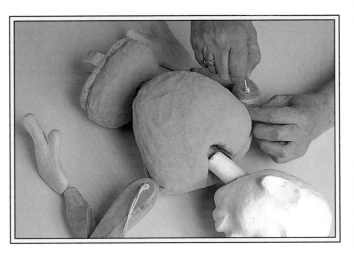

5 *Drill a hole through the top of each arm. Join each arm to the body: thread cord through the hole in the body, thread both ends through the hole in the top of the arm, then knot the ends together. Seal the knots with glue.*

MAKING THE LEGS AND HIP JOINTS

The knees are made using the same kind of joint as you used for the elbows. The legs may be made either entirely from wood or from plywood and foam rubber as shown here. This second method means that the legs then have the right kind of bulk, but are not heavy, which is ideal.

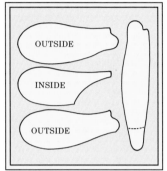

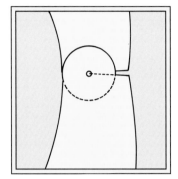

1 Cut leg shapes out of paper, following the patterns shown, in a size and shape appropriate to your puppet, leaving a little extra at the end of the lower leg to fit into the foot to make the ankle joint.

2 Transfer the patterns for the upper leg to a sheet of plywood and cut them out using a coping saw or jigsaw. Repeat this for the lower leg, using very slightly thinner plywood.

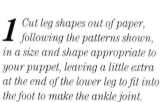

3 Glue together the three thigh sections, creating as you do so a slot to accommodate the top of the lower leg. Insert this tongue into the slot and drill through the leg at the center point of the overlapping parts. As you did with the elbow joint, remove the lower leg, enlarge the hole slightly, then reassemble the joint and insert a

nail. When the knee joint moves freely, secure the nail with a spot of glue on its head.

4 Glue pieces of foam rubber to the plywood and trim them to the right shape (take care that the foam rubber does not impede the movement of the knee joint).

5 To make the hip joints, drill a hole through the top of each leg and through the leg spacer built into the pelvis. Insert a piece of galvanized wire (coathanger wire) through the legs and spacer. Bend the ends of the wire upward at a sharp angle and bend the tops

in to fit into holes pre-drilled in the pelvis; then secure the ends of the wire in place with glue. The wire needs to be bent to form a sharp angle because if it were a smooth curve, the legs might slip along the wire and become wedged at an awkward angle.

MAKING THE FEET

The feet are made from wood to which detail may be added using plastic wood if necessary.

1 Using a saw, chisel, rasp and/or craft knife, carve out the basic foot shape from a block of wood.

3 When it has hardened, build up or cut away the plastic wood as necessary and finish as described for the plastic wood head and hands.

2 You may cover the surfaces of the wood with clear contact glue and press on plastic wood, shaping it as you do so.

MAKING THE ANKLE JOINT

The ankle joint is made by cutting a slot in the foot, into which the plywood projection on the bottom of the leg fits.

1 Drill a series of holes exactly next to each other down near the heel end of the foot to create a slot.

3 Slide the leg projection into the slot and drill a small hole through the ankle and the projection at the mid-point.

2 Use a craft knife to cut out the rest of the wood in the slot until you have a smooth-sided channel.

4 Remove the projection, enlarge the hole in it slightly as you did for the elbows and knees, then reassemble the joint. Insert a nail through the joint and secure the head of the nail with a drop of glue.

PAINTING AND DRESSING THE PUPPET

Paint the head, hands and feet at the same time so that colors match, and add the costume.

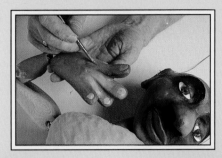

1 *Quick hemming is achieved by running a line of glue along the edge of the material and then turning it up. Before gluing fabrics together, the visible edge must be neat and prevented from fraying: run a thin line of glue and spread it along the edge with your finger. In a few moments, when the glue is dry, trim the edge as necessary with scissors.*

2 *Make sleeves or pants by gluing the fabric into tubes. For sleeves, the tops are shaped to fit onto the body; they are often glued on after the fabric on the body, but either way is possible. For pants the tops of the fabric tubes are left open and glued together around the pelvis. You might need to clip into the edges of the fabric at the crotch in order to open out the top of the pants sufficiently.*

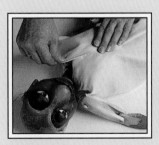

3 *This puppet's shirt is being tailored directly onto the body in sections which are trimmed to shape as each piece is attached. If the puppet were to have a jacket, only the front and collar of the shirt would be needed. Here a shirt is fitted by laying the puppet on the fabric, which is folded around the body* *and trimmed to shape, then glued on. A separate fly front hides the join.*

4 *The sleeves and collar are glued to the shirt separately.*

5 *The pants are glued to the shirt and a waistband or belt covers the join.*

Your marionette is now ready to have its control and strings added.

MAKING AN UPRIGHT CONTROL

An upright control is an inverted wooden cross to which a dowel shoulder bar, hand control wires and a removable leg bar are attached.

All dowels are up to ⅜in (9mm) in diameter. The vertical bar is a piece of wood measuring 9 × 1 × 1in (23 × 2.5 × 2.5cm). The head bar is made from 1 × 1in (2.5 × 2.5cm) wood. They are joined, as shown, by means of a cross-halving joint.

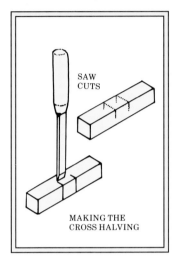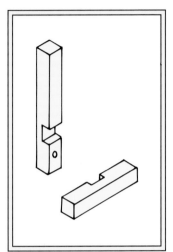

SAW CUTS

MAKING THE CROSS HALVING

1 *Cut halfway down through each piece of wood in two places, making the distance between the cuts the exact width of the other piece, and exactly in the middle of the short piece of wood.*

2 *Chisel out the wood between the cuts until you have a smooth, even channel; then glue and interlock the two pieces to form a sturdy cross. Secure with a screw if necessary.*

3 *Drill a hole for the shoulder bar midway between the head bar and the bottom of the control. This bar is approximately 5in (12.5cm) long (it must be long enough to hold the shoulder strings away from the head and not impede movement). Glue the end of the bar into the hole so that it sticks out at the back. It must be a tight fit and may be secured with a small nail through the side of the control if necessary.*

4 *To attach a leg bar, fit a screw-eye into the center of a piece of* *dowel about 8in (20cm) long and suspend it from a hook near the top of the control.*

5 *Make the hand controls from galvanized wire (coathanger wire) and long enough to rest on the head bar when they are finished (usually this is about level with the bottom of the control). Drill two small holes for them horizontally through the control bar, one above the other and ³⁄₈in (1cm) apart. Make sure that they are sufficiently below the leg bar not to interfere with it. Use pliers to bend a short length at the end of each wire into a right angle. Insert the other ends of the wire through the holes in opposite directions.*

Carefully bend these ends down with pliers, but do not make them fit too tightly to the upright or they will not move freely. Also, make the angles as sharp as possible as curves will mean that they will wobble. To achieve a good, sharp angle when you are bending the wire down, keep a firm pressure upward against the short horizontal piece. This takes a little practice. Next cut the wires to the same length and make loops in the ends to which the hand strings will be attached later. Seal the loops with clear contact glue.

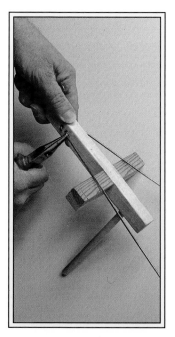

6 *Drill holes through the ends of the head, leg and shoulder bars just large enough to thread the strings through. Drill a hole for the back string 2in (5cm) from the end of the shoulder bar.*

7 *With the edge of a file, make a groove around the ends of all bars where thread is to be attached. This will make it easier to secure the strings later.*

8 *Finely sand the whole control assembly smooth because rough edges will fray the strings.*

STRINGING THE MARIONETTE

For stringing use black Dacron braided nylon fishing line (strength 10lb) or a comparable substitute. Before stringing, wax the thread with beeswax as this will strengthen it, reducing fraying or breaking. Rub the strings thereafter from time to time to lengthen their life. Beware of nylon thread: it tends to stretch, glistens under lights, drawing attention to itself, and retains crinkles if it is wound up while the puppet is not in use.

When you are attaching the strings to the control bars, before knotting them, wind them around the grooves you filed in the bars.

String the puppet when it is in a standing position. It is best to fix a strong hook in some suitable place and hang from it a piece of chain so that the control can be hooked into it at any height. Put a table or chair under the chain for the puppet to stand on.

When you are transporting your marionette, wind its strings around winders – rectangles cut from plywood or hardboard and slotted, then sanded – to prevent them from becoming tangled.

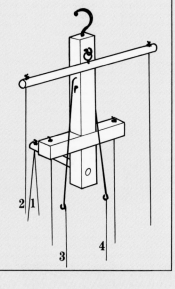

1 SHOULDER STRING

2 LEG STRING

3 HEAD STRING

4 HAND STRING

1 *Attach the head strings first to establish the height of the control. Make the strings long enough for the puppet to stand on the stage when the control is held at elbow height. Either drill small holes through the tops of the ears or secure the strings to small screw-eyes screwed into the dowel built into the head. Make sure that the strings are of equal length so that the head is level.*

2 *Attach the shoulder and back strings to the screw-eyes secured in the shoulder blades and back of the pelvis, using a needle to pass the thread through the costume, then through the screw-eye. Secure the other ends of the threads to the shoulder bar. The back string should be a little loose so that the puppet can move freely. Adjust the tension between head and shoulder strings as necessary so that the head is held in the right position in relation to the body.*

3 *Make the hand strings just long enough for the hands to hang by the puppet's sides when the controls rest on the head bar. Drill a small hole through an appropriate place in each hand, depending on how you wish the hand to be held (for example, through to the back of the hand, through the thumb, between the thumb and knuckle of the index finger). With a larger drill bit, countersink the hole to hide the knot. Tie the string to the loop in the hand control wire, then thread the other end through the hole in the hand and knot the end.*

4 *For the leg strings, drill holes through the legs just above the knees, and with a needle push the thread through and knot the ends, ensuring that the knots do not impede the movement of the legs. Make the strings just long enough to allow you to unhook the bar without moving the legs.*

5 *When all the strings have been tied securely, seal the knots using clear contact glue and trim the ends of the threads close to the knots to finish them.*

Hold the main control in one hand, taking the weight of the puppet on your middle, ring and little fingers. If you find it comfortable, hold your little finger under the head bar, but if you do not, hold it above the bar.

Use your thumb and index fingers to move the hand wires and your free hand to operate the leg bar as well as any strings that need to be lifted individually.

To nod or bow the head, tilt the control forward. To lean the head to one side, tilt the control sideways. To turn the head, tilt the control very slightly forward, just enough to take the weight on the shoulder strings, at the same time turning the control.

To move the hands, raise or lower the hand wires with your thumb or index finger. This, though, provides limited control so, for further movement, manipulate the strings directly, together or separately, with your free hand.

To make the puppet walk, unhook the leg bar with your free hand and move it in a paddling motion. Keep the main control moving in unison and try to achieve some rhythm to its movement to accompany the movement of the legs. With just a little practice you will soon find that you can achieve a rhythm, with the momentum of the legs doing most of the walking action for you. Take care not to let the legs swing like pendula, with the feet not touching the ground, nor to let the puppet walk as though it were sitting down! You will soon feel when the puppet is walking well, and you will know when it is just touching the floor because it will feel very slightly lighter.

You do not need to re-hook the leg bar to the main control bar to free a hand to work other strings. With your ring and little fingers, just hold it against your palm, leaving your middle and index fingers and thumb free. You can then keep the leg bar in your hand all the time.

To achieve convincing manipulation, watch how people move. For example, see how they lean forward to retain their balance while moving from sitting to standing and vice versa. Practice such movements with your puppet. You might use a mirror for practice, but be careful not to become dependent on the mirror, or you will find it harder to perform without it. You need to develop a feel for what the puppet is doing and when it is moving well. Video can be very helpful for studying and improving your technique without having to use a mirror.

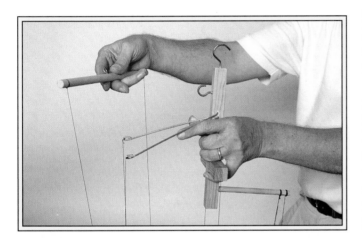

5

Staging and Performance

–

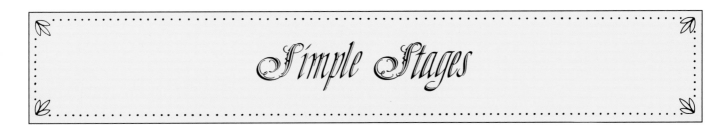

Simple Stages

Stages may be improvised very quickly for use at home or elsewhere. For example, suitably draped, a three-sided clothes horse can be used for presenting all types of puppet shows, an large cardboard boxes are easily converted into stages.

A CARDBOARD STAGE

This simple stage can be very effective for three-dimensional puppets.

1 Find a large, sturdy cardboard box and cut off the top flaps and one side. Leave two of the bottom flaps turned inward and bend the middle flap forward to help steady the theater. If necessary, place a heavy weight on the inside flaps to steady the stage, or secure it to the table top with masking tape.

2 You can leave the top edge of the box straight and add scenery as required, or you can cut a design into the box itself.

3 Decorate the box with paint, fabric or wallpaper as you like.

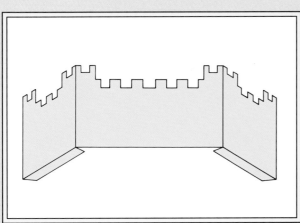

SCENERY

Scenery slots enable you to add scenery and change the appearance of the stage. This adds atmosphere and gives the puppets a context in which to perform.

1 Glue two squares of strong cardboard, suitably spaced, to the inside of the stage. Glue a rectangular piece of cardboard to the squares to form a slot for holding the scenery.

2 Cut out cardboard scenery with a tongue on the bottom so that it fits into the scenery slot.

3 If you add a series of scenery slots to the stage, you can use them to secure a large scene-setting piece, but make sure that the tongues align with the slots.

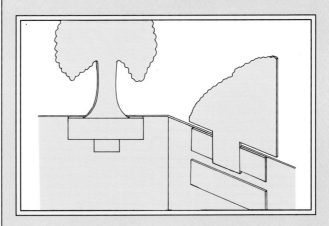

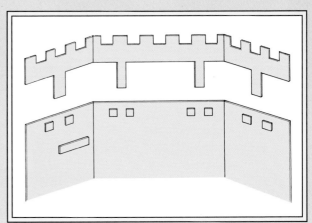

A Simple Shadow Puppet Theater

The cardboard stage design may be adapted for use with shadow puppets. Normally the puppets are operated from behind with horizontal controls. If you wish to project scenery, operation from below is necessary. Make the frame from a large box with enough space below the screen for you to operate without obstructing the light. Suitable materials for the screen are described on page 75.

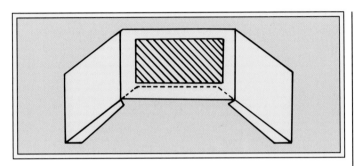

1 *In the center section, cut a hole for the screen, leaving space at each side and plenty of space below. Using glue or masking tape,* *fasten the screen over the inside of the hole, pulling the screen taut so that it does not sag or wrinkle.*

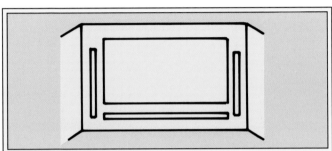

3 *Cut three narrow strips of cardboard that are the same thickness as the scenery, making one strip a little longer than the screen opening and two* *approximately the same as its height. Glue them below and to the sides of the screen as shown, leaving at least 1in (2.5cm) between the strips and the screen opening.*

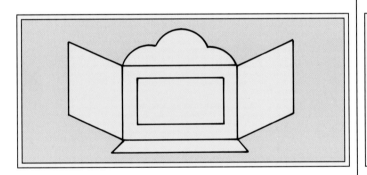

2 *Use the side you removed to make a decorative top-piece to hide the operator(s). You can glue it to the frame or, if you use the theatre for other types of puppets,* *attach the top piece by means of scenery slots as described opposite. Decorate the theater using paints, fabric, wallpaper or other materials to achieve the effect you want.*

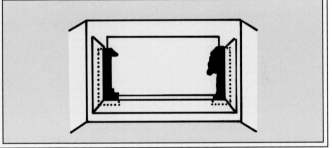

4 *Cut out and glue to these strips three wider pieces of cardboard with mitered corners to frame the opening. The inside* *edges should be just clear of the screen opening, creating a slot or pocket around the screen into which the scenery can be placed.*

A PICTURE FRAME SHADOW THEATER

An alternative shadow theater is quickly made by securing suitable fabric (page 75) to a picture frame using a staple gun, thumbtacks or masking tape. Attach the frame to a wooden base (such as an old shelf) by means of two L-shaped brackets. If side curtains are needed, screw a wooden batten to the top of the picture frame and suspend the drapes from the batten.

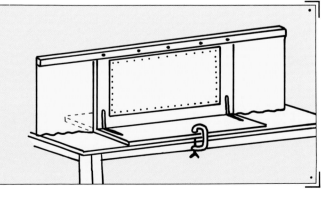

A Wooden Table-Top Theater

DIMENSIONS AND MATERIALS

The dimensions of the theater will depend on your needs, including the number of operators there will be and allowing enough space for the puppets to perform without being too restricted. I recommend that the minimum dimensions should be 39½in wide by 27½in high (100cm wide by 70cm high).

For the stage and frame, use 2 × 1in (50 × 25mm) lumber that is 1¾ × ¾in (45 × 18mm) planed all around, approximately ⅜-in (9-mm) diameter doweling, and ¾-in (18-mm) blockboard. Use woodworking glue as the adhesive. See below for the shapes of all of the parts and how they fit together.

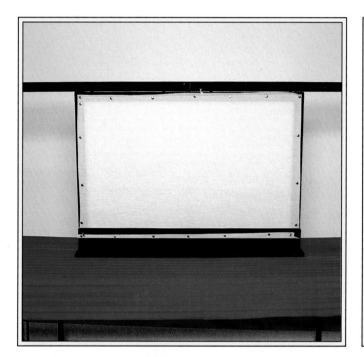

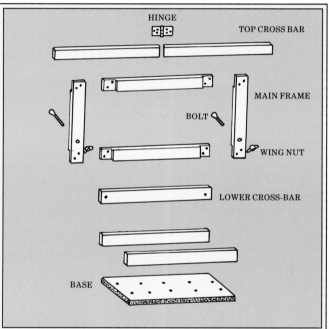

1 Make the frame for a shadow screen by gluing and screwing together four lengths of wood with half-lap joints at the corners. Make sure that the corners are true.

2 Make the base by gluing and screwing two lengths of the wood to the blockboard (countersink the holes for the screws so that the heads are flush with the chipboard). To ensure that the timber is appropriately spaced to hold the frame securely, use the bottom of the frame as a spacer during construction.

3 Fit the frame into the slot created on the base. If it does not fit snugly, secure it with two bolts and wing nuts as shown. Lay another length of wood on top of the base to form a lower cross bar. Drill a hole through each end of the cross bar and the two uprights. Secure the cross bar to the rear of the frame with bolts and wing nuts after attaching the shadow screen to the frame.

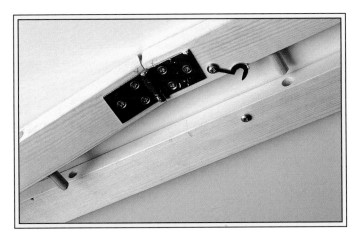

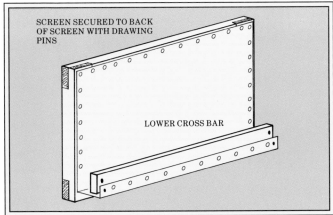

SCREEN SECURED TO BACK OF SCREEN WITH DRAWING PINS

LOWER CROSS BAR

4 Use a long piece of lumber to make the curtain pole. It may be hinged if necessary. To attach the pole to the frame, cut four ½in (12mm) diameter dowel pegs, each 3in (7.5cm) long. Position the curtain pole on top of the frame and clamp the two together securely. Drill four holes down through the curtain pole and the frame. Glue the dowel pegs into the holes in the pole so that the protruding ends of the dowels fit into the holes in the top of the frame. The weight of the pole holds it in place, and it can be removed simply by lifting it off.

5 If the curtain bar is hinged, you might need to add a small hook near the center of the bar to hold it tightly against the frame, which is important because this bar is the playing level for hand and rod puppets.

6 Attach your chosen shadow screen material to the back of the frame with thumbtacks. Fix it at the top and side, keeping it taut. Pass it under the lower cross bar and pin it to the side facing the operator.

7 The lower cross bar provides a ledge on which shadow puppets may walk, and the space between the bar and the screen makes a useful slot for holding scenery.

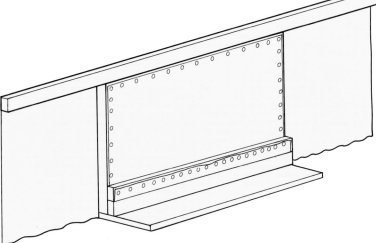

8 Attach the drapes to the curtain bar. These may be gathered and pinned to the curtain bar or suspended from a curtain wire or glide rail attached to the bar. A wire or rail allows the curtains to be opened and closed across the screen, using a cording set to produce the amount of movement you want. Being able to close the curtains is useful if you wish to use the theater for all types of puppet.

Operate hand and rod puppets behind and above the curtain pole. Play shadow puppets against the shadow screen and marionettes over the curtain bar.

THE SHADOW SCREEN

Use a semi-opaque material for the screen. A piece of white polyester/cotton sheeting is satisfactory. Architects' tracing sheet gives a clear image, but tracing linen is stronger and preferable. White shower-curtain fabric is excellent. Also recommended is a Cinemoid lighting acetate called frost, which should be used with the matt surface facing the audience.

Keep the screen taut; if it sags or wrinkles, it will mar the performance.

It is a good idea to construct your stage from units that can be assembled in a variety of ways. Rectangular units made to two or three common dimensions are the most helpful as you can then match the parts as you like. A mixture of single and hinged units are recommended to facilitate quick assembly.

The units shown are made from sections 36in high by 30in wide (90 × 75cm) hinged together. There are also a few center panels measuring 36 × 48in (90 × 120cm).

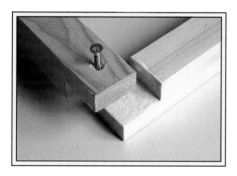

1 *For strength and stability, use 1½ × 1½in (38 × 38mm) wood joined with half-lap joints, glued and screwed together.*

2 *Finely sand all edges and then clad the frames with a suitable material before hinging the parts together. Attach the fabric with glue and a staple gun, taking care with the corners.*

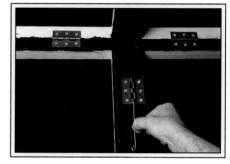

3 *The frames are hinged together to create book-style units. Use loose-pin hinges to join separate units. Position them very carefully so that they all align, or the units will not be interchangeable. Hold the units open with triangular plywood plates, cut to fit the corners and bolted on as shown in the booth below.*

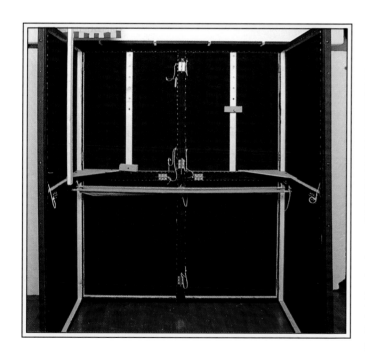

You can adapt the stage to any type of puppet. For example, this glove and rod puppet booth may incorporate a shadow screen. It has a back-screen (supported by three battens bolted to the back of the booth), a plywood playboard for props on stage (slotted for items on rods) and a fabric cradle attached to rods for a props shelf.

You do not always need a stage. Marionettes may perform in the open, with no stage or a minimal stage constructed from units with additions as required. A simple but effective design is illustrated. Wing units are helpful to hide backstage activity. Marionettes need a suitable floor covering to walk on, such as thin carpet, burlap or felt in order to reduce noise and prevent the puppet from slipping as it walks.

You will also need a back rail on which to hang the marionettes "backstage": a strong and secure design is illustrated. It uses an A-frame for each end; they are held rigid by crossed lengths of wood bolted to the frame. Aluminum tubing is used for the hanging rail: it is held in holes drilled through the tops of the A-frames.

SCENERY, LIGHTING AND SOUND

1 *Batik backscreen.*
2 *A sliding scenery slot.*
3 *Backstage view.*
4 *The performance*

SCENERY

Simplicity is the key to effective scenery. Back screens may be plain drapes, say a light blue sky cloth, fabric collage, dyed fabric (sponged, tie-dyed or batik) or painted plywood. Try relief sculpting or modeling on a plywood base with the materials described in the Introduction; this is effective, too.

Attach the backcloth to a batten. The batten is joined to the back frame by T-shaped metal brackets bent into hooks.

Glue and screw large scenery to a batten which attaches to the framework. Inverted keyhole shapes in the batten, hooked over screws in the framework, make possible quick changes of scenery. You will need to drill holes in the other half of the unit to accommodate the screws for when you wish to fold up the frames.

Attach smaller pieces of scenery to the stage by means of a sliding scenery slot, so that scenery can be raised and lowered smoothly without revealing your hands. Glue and screw together three strips of plywood or fiberboard with spacers in between to create two slots as shown. One slot fits over the "slide" which is screwed to the main frame. The other slot carries a wooden tongue attached to the bottom of the scenery.

Insert the scenery tongue into the slot and drill a hole through the carrier and the scenery tongue and into the wooden slide. Insert a ½-in (12-mm) diameter dowel peg into the hole to secure the scenery. Attach the dowel to the frame with cord.

If you wish to use a playboard with sliding slot scenery, you must set the playboard back a little from the front of the stage to allow enough space for the scenery to pass through.

LIGHTING

For small performances you may not need, or have space for, special lighting. If you do require it, keep it simple to enhance the performance and not obscure visibility: try to avoid dimly lit scenes, as the puppet theatre usually needs more light than human theatre. For anything other than large-scale or professional shows, the kind of spotlights and floodlights found in normal households are adequate. You can attach them to the stage or to extension arms bolted to the stage, but it is best if they are not too close to the puppets. Separate telescopic stands or attachments at other suitable locations are preferable.

Side lights, cross-lighting the stage, are the most common: two lights are the minimum to highlight modeling and eliminate heavy shadows. For a stage 10 feet (3 meters) wide, puppeteers would use three or four lights on each side, but approach color lighting with caution: visibility is paramount. For effective color lighting, you would need several lights with different-color filters and separate dimmer controls, as changing filters on hot lights during a show is difficult.

If you do require more professional lighting, most stage-lighting manufacturers make compact lights (prism convex, pebble convex, fresnels and floodlights) which are ideal for puppet theaters, provided you have somewhere to anchor them.

LIGHTING FOR SHADOW PUPPETS

Shadows may be performed without blackout or artificial light. If lighting is used, however, just one light is needed (except for special effects), as two light sources will cause blurred images.

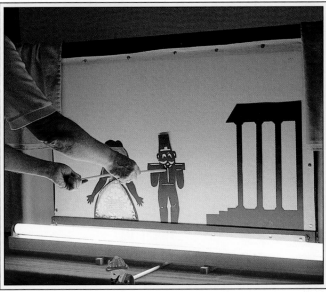

1 Daylight is often adequate: simply position the screen so that it backs onto a window. The puppets will show, but the operators and control rods will not. Avoid standing in strong sunlight, however, as you will cast unwanted shadows.

2 A fluorescent tube on a suitable base can be placed behind the screen; this provides good, diffused light, shows neither performers nor control rods, and remains cool; and color filters can be laid across the light to create different moods.

3 A gooseneck lamp is sufficient. Simply stand it at the side of the screen so that it does not interfere with manipulation.

4 An overhead projector or slide projector gives crisp light and allows scenery to be projected onto your screen. Moving the puppets toward the light also enlarges the image. Use vertical control wires if you choose this option or you will block the light when you perform.

SOUND

If needed, a sound system may range from an audio-cassette player to a cassette tape deck with amplifier, microphone and loudspeakers, or an integral sound system like a simple *karaoke* unit.

DEVELOPING A PLAY

Let the puppets do that which *they* do well and not what human theater does *better*. Puppets should bring something of their own to the performance, not present a trivial version. Much puppet theater originates from narrative because human plays often rely heavily on the word, but puppets need action to be effective, so consider how much of the story can be translated into action.

Make a schedule for the entire production and stick to it, or you will find that you can easily spend too long on construction and be short of rehearsal time.

Develop a scenario, an outline of the action, including basic stage directions. Make sure that all the important action takes place on stage. In doing this you might need to eliminate or combine some characters and limit the action to three or four scenes. Also, keep the stage clear of nonessential characters and the number of operators to a minimum.

Having identified the major aspects of the scenario, develop the links so that the play flows and continuity is maintained. Then write the script or record, transcribe and edit an improvisation with puppets. Use substitutes if the puppets themselves are not ready, as human acting is not a good basis for puppet acting. Make sure, too, that the dialogue challenges rather than patronizes the audience.

MUSIC AND VOICE

Music should add to the atmosphere, not draw too much attention to itself. It is usual to precede curtain-up with music to set the mood, but it may detract from the finale if it is used after the final curtain.

Voice work depends upon posture, proper breathing and good projection. Use live rather than recorded voices if at all possible. The quality is significantly different, and taped dialogue cannot allow for all audience reactions or for technical hitches. Also, learn your lines – you cannot read *and* perform.

OPERATING THE PUPPETS

Try to make the puppet convincing in its role and, within the limits of characterization, explore a wide variety of movements. Like your voice, the puppet's gestures should be crisp, clean and clearly delineated. Economy of gesture is a good basic rule. Do one thing at a time and start a new move when there is a new thought. The late John Wright maintained: "Every line should have an action and every action should have a meaning. Never put in unnecessary movement." Pace is important, too: think quickly, but do not hurry; take your time.

So that the audience can tell who is speaking, relate the actions of the puppet to the words, but do not jiggle it about to every syllable of speech. Use the puppet's movements to emphasize important words or phrases and subdue slightly the actions of the other characters, without leaving them lifeless.

Consider, too, entrances and exits. The puppet must be moving in character *before* it appears and not simply drop in or pop up on to the stage as this destroys the illusion.

REHEARSALS

First, establish the overall patterns of movement (known as *blocking*) and note them in the master script. Next, determine the actions of individual characters, then detailed movement, so that the puppet's movements flow cleanly from one position or motif to the next. Finally, put all the elements together again and rehearse it adequately as a whole, perfecting your technique and, at the same time, building your confidence.

Most puppet shows are too long, so be disciplined about the length of the show. Avoid long scene changes: the absolute maximum is two to three minutes. If possible, let the performers take turns to watch rehearsals and use video to study your performance from the audience's point of view.

When you have perfected all this, you are ready. Good luck, and enjoy your performance! Then review and strengthen it in the light of audience response and enjoy it more and more.

The author would like to extend thanks to the following:
To Ian Howes who photographed all construction aspects, making helpful
suggestions and providing practical assistance, and also for his
entertaining tales, good humor and friendship; to Ian's daughter Pippa
Howes whose artistic talents for modeling and painting have helped to
make the puppets look so splendid; to Emma Covell and Terry Roberts for
help with puppets and stages; to Martin Norris who photographed the
finished puppets and performance set-ups; to the Puppet Centre in
London and Georgina Stein of the Primary Technology Centre,
Roehampton Institute; to Stefanie Foster, Editor, Richard Dewing, Art
Director, and the production team at Quintet. And not least to my wife,
Ayla, who has provided all manner of support.
Thank you Ayla.

Sources of Information

Britain

The Puppet Centre Trust
Battersea Arts Centre
Lavender Hill
London SW11 5TN
Director: Cath March

Scottish Mask and Puppet Centre
8 Balcarres Avenue
Kelvindale
Glasgow G12 0QF
Director: Malcolm Knight

UNIMA (Union Internationale de la Marionnette)

The international puppetry organization founded in 1929 which
"unites the puppeteers of the world" has branches in many
countries. For information contact one of the following:

Australia

Australian Centre of UNIMA
Coonarra Road
Olinda
Victoria 3788

Britain

Ray DaSilva
Hon. Secretary, British UNIMA
The Limes
Norwich Road
Marsham
Norfolk NR10 5PS

Canada

Pierre Tremblay
Association Quebecoise des
  Marionnettistes
Case Postale 7
Succ de Lorimier
Montreal
Quebec H2H 2N6

or

Don Rubin
York University
4700 Keele Street
North York
Ontario M3J 1P3

Ireland

Miriam Lambert
Irish UNIMA
5 Clifton Terrace
Monkstown
Co. Dublin

New Zealand

UNIMA New Zealand
9 Denman Street
Christchurch 8

South Africa

National Centre of UNIMA
1 Magnet Street
Kensington
Johannesburg 2094

U.S.A.

Allelu Kurten
UNIMA General Secretary
Browning Road
Hyde Park
New York 12538

Information correct at
time of going to print